SUCCESS, HEALTH, AND HAPPINESS

The Epigrams of B.J. Palmer

INTEGRAL ALTITUDE

INTEGRAL ALTITUDE is dedicated to publishing important books and media, which shed new light on topics such as chiropractic, spirituality, wellness, enlightenment, philosophy, integral theory, and subtle energies. The series is designed to foster new ideas and to publish previously forgotten materials, seeds of today's new ways of thinking and being.

MORE TITLES FROM INTEGRAL ALTITUDE

THE SPIRITUAL WRITINGS OF BJ PALMER
The Second Chiropractor
Simon A. Senzon

THE SECRET HISTORY OF CHIROPRACTIC
D.D. Palmer's Spiritual Writings
Simon A. Senzon, Foreword by Guy Riekeman

CHIROPRACTIC FOUNDATIONS
D.D. Palmer's Traveling Library
Simon A. Senzon

A TEXTBOOK: MODERNIZED CHIROPRACTIC (2007/1906)
With a new introduction by *Simon A. Senzon*
Minora Paxson, Oakley Smith, & Solon Langworthy

THE CHIROPRACTIC VISION (DVD)
Simon A. Senzon

THE LIFE AND TIMES OF BJ PALMER (AUDIO BOOK)
Simon A. Senzon

SUCCESS, HEALTH, AND HAPPINESS

The Epigrams of B.J. Palmer

by
SIMON A. SENZON

Integral Altitude
Asheville, N.C.

First Edition 2010

Published in the United States by Integral Altitude
218 E. Chestnut St. Asheville, N.C. 28801

Senzon, Simon, b. 1971
    Success, Health, and Happiness: The Epigrams of B.J. Palmer / by Simon A. Senzon.
    1st ed.

Includes bibliographical references.
    Summary: "B.J. Palmer's epigrams written in the 20th century are a source of inspiration and humor. Palmer was one of the least known and most influential individuals in American history. Palmer was a true genius and enlightened thinker. His epigrams will inspire readers for generations to come."--Provided by publisher.

ISBN 978-0-9827244-0-8 (pbk)

Manufactured in the United States of America 10 9 8 7 6 5 4 3 2 1

For current information about all releases from Integral Altitude, visit the web site at
http://www.philosophyofchiropractic.com

This book is dedicated to my father, Ivan Lance Senzon (1943-2009)

Why these epigrams?

What is before you, is seen.
What is being seen, is read.
What is being read, is thot.
What is being thot, is acted.

What is acted, is YOU.

—BJ Palmer
As a Man Thinketh

B. J. PALMER, D. C., Ph. C.

Developer of Chiropractic

CONTENTS

PREFACE

This book is about life and living.

When I decided to put this book together, my intention was to share these incredible, inspiring, witty, and often funny epigrams with the world. These epigrams have inspired thousands of my friends and colleagues for over fifty years. And yet very few people have read them. I knew that by categorizing Palmer's epigrams, the wisdom, practical advice, and humor would become easily available for the first time. The book soon developed into one of the great keys to living a good life.

The categories grew into twenty-three chapters. Instead of just writing an introduction to each chapter, I chose to highlight Palmer's philosophy of life. In his later years, Palmer viewed each person as a reflection of the divine wisdom at the heart of the universe. Individuals could tap this unlimited potential within by allowing the inner intelligence to guide them in life. Through flashes of inspiration, seeming synchronicity, or just following through on one's own innate greatness in work, relationship, body, mind, heart, and spirit, incredible genius and creative fulfillment becomes possible. Most of the introductions center on quotes from Palmer describing how to access your own potential.

Finally, I have included an epilogue detailing Palmer's own development during the course of his life. It is one thing to read the sayings and glean wisdom from the philosophy. It is another to be inspired by actions and to watch how one person confronts each new challenge in life as a crucible, a defining moment. With each of these crucibles, Palmer developed himself. He used hard times and life challenges to thrive in each new phase of life. His philosophy and his sayings can be viewed as the product of a life being lived to the fullest.

This book is the result of love and support from many individuals and organizations. I am grateful for the generous help and loving support of Sherri McClendon, Matt Rentschler, Susanne Cook-Greuter, Ken Wilber, Alana Callendar, Glenda Wiese, Kathy Woods, Dan Lemberger, Cynthia Hynes, Donny and Jackie Epstein, Dominique Hort, Pierre Bernier, Michelle McCarthy, William and Carole Peyton, Jack Senzon, Michelle Anderson, and many friends and colleagues around the world.

A special thanks to *The Journal of Integral Theory and Practice* for allowing me to publish the epilogue on the life of B.J. Palmer even before it goes to print in the journal. The epilogue was supported by a grant from the Global Gateway Foundation. The grant was meant to support projects furthering the mission of the foundation.

Thank you so much to Thom Gelardi for writing the foreword.

I am so thankful for my mother, Roni Senzon and all of her love and support for the past 39 years! Mom, you are an inspiration to me.

I am also eternally grateful to my son Noah and my daughter Arielle, two of the most wonderful children a father could ask for.

To my wife Susan – you are awesome. I appreciate all that you do. Thank you!

And to you the reader, thank you.

Simon A. Senzon

Asheville, NC

April 2010

FOREWORD

Recently, my sister and I were reminiscing about our parents, and she remarked how our father frequently used aphorisms in his conversations. I can hear him now saying, "God helps those who help themselves" and "You can achieve anything you want, if you want bad enough." I believe Dad and his aphorisms influenced my life far more than he ever imagined.

I don't know whether it was inheriting a few of Dad's genes or being exposed to his predilections, but I certainly have a great appreciation for aphorisms and epigrams. While in college, I read Norman Vincent Peal's book, *The Power of Positive Thinking*, wherein he recommended that one fill their mind with aphorisms and call upon selected ones as needed. That habit has served me well through the years. If I could not find one appropriate to a recurring situation, I would compose my own. During challenging times, I would remind myself that the measure of a man is what it takes to get him down. Or when inclined to self-pity, I would advise myself to either lie down and give up or get up and go, but not waste time and energy hanging around the middle ground.

My life has been greatly influenced by the philosophers, no less by B.J. Palmer. It is said when the student is ready the teacher appears; perhaps I was ready. Through my father's advice, I came at an early age to believe in the power of self-discipline, and that I was here for a purpose. As a young person, plagued with health problems and unaware of the label "vitalism," I innately believed my body had the intelligence to maintain its own health. I also believed life is purposeful and moves forward. So, I was ready for B.J.

Dr. B. J. Palmer, or just B. J. as he preferred, was a renaissance man in both knowledge and deed. He was not a complex or conflicted person. He was a rather simple man, grounded in a philosophy, which held that a person could tap into their infinite innate mind as a source of wisdom and guidance. Listening to his innate wisdom drove him and gave him the knowledge to do the many and varied things he undertook. I wonder if B.J.'s innate mind was the source for the synthesis of information already stored in his photographic memory. His practical and logical mind was filled with data from many fields, including anatomy, physiology, clinical chiropractic, philosophy, anthropology, speleology, history, literature, and archaeology. His writings on self-reliance and the work ethic parallel those of Emerson and Elbert Hubbard.

B.J. also loved the business of movies, radio, and television. He chartered WOC, the second radio station in the U.S. and the first to sell commercial time. His book *Radio Salesmanship* became a standard college textbook for effectively writing on-air communications.

He wrote some 30 volumes, many of them on chiropractic philosophical and clinical subjects. Others were on a wide variety of topics, ranging from the lost civilizations in Cambodia to the Shakespeare-Bacon controversy to theories of reincarnation. His books, along with items for his chiropractic school and his radio/television companies, were printed at his own printing and publishing company. He was president of the Palmer School of Chiropractic and Director of the B. J. Palmer Chiropractic Research Clinic and the Clearview Sanitarium.

He served for several terms as president of the International Chiropractor's Association and lectured worldwide.

When I entered the Palmer School of Chiropractic in January of 1954, I found just about every inch of each wall covered with epigrams. They were on the outside of the buildings, in the stairwells, above the urinals in the men's room, and even on the walls of the elevator shafts. One could not help but read them, and through repeatedly seeing them they became part of one's thoughts and one's self.

Above each doorway entering the campus buildings were the words, "Enter to Learn How" and on the leaving side of the doorways were the words, "Go Forth and Serve." I found we students also learned the why, something as important as the how. It was because of the why I have tried to dedicate my life to serving.

Influenced as much by B.J.'s example as from his powerful lectures, I carried away from his teachings an understanding of the great wisdom running through our bodies. Whether it is called "innate intelligence," as he preferred, or just *nature,* as it is commonly understood, this concept perceived in all living things, has a fundamental self-interest.

B.J. may not have been the first to influence me. Regarding the core of his philosophy however, in regards to "the student being ready," he was. His concept of the Innate Intelligence having one mission; to look after the matter (the body and life) in which it resides was new. It was consistent with the idea of self-interest being normal and natural, and comfortable. This fit with my core beliefs. I learned to give all patients, regardless of their station in life or ability to pay the best care possible, and believe this has much to do with the doctor's health, self-esteem, stress level, charisma, prosperity, and joy of living.

Not only were epigrams on the walls, but B. J. spoke epigrammatically. We frequently heard his deep sonorous voice advise us, "Get the Big Idea; all else follows" or "We never know how far reaching something we may think, say, or do today will affect the lives of millions tomorrow."

I consider myself most fortunate to have attended Palmer School of Chiropractic during the time B. J. was its president. The profession was only about fifty years old at the time, and it was experiencing the pains and joy of bringing this new teaching and service to the world. Chiropractic was not a career choice, it was a mission. Indeed, B. J.'s "Spizzerinctum!",[1] was everywhere.

Not everyone in the profession loved B. J. Some had difficulty accepting his strict adherence to putting principle above personality, of having the clinical and social advancement of chiropractic the standard for determining the value of his every decision, and his uncompromising effort to maintain the integrity of chiropractic as a separate and distinct profession. But, whether one loved or hated him, everyone agreed that his leadership was essential for chiropractic's early meteoric growth throughout the world.

Those who knew B.J. more intimately than I confirm what I gleaned from my experience; B.J. was a very ethical person. He had a great belief that infallible natural law determined personal success as it did personal health, and that acting ethically and virtuously were indispensible parts of those cycles.

The Palmer School was situated on most of a city block in Davenport, Iowa. Among the few exceptions to Palmer buildings on the block was a Catholic Convent. A number of nuns, brothers and priests were chiropractic practice members, and some attended B.J.'s public lectures. I recall attending one of those lectures. I had to wonder how the clergy felt when B. J. said, "All religions are man-made and I'm the man who made my religion." From his lectures and writings, it seems to be that B.J.'s spiritual persuasion was similar to Einstein's pantheism or Thomas Jefferson's deism.

Betty, my wife, once mentioned to Dr. Agnes Palmer, B.J.'s daughter-in-law, how impressed we were with the writings of Ayn Rand. Before she could tell her that I was requiring students in my philosophy class to read *The Fountainhead,* Agnes said that B.J. had required his students to read *The Fountainhead* in *his* philosophy course. I could easily understand B.J. appreciating Ayn Rand's rationalism and objectivist philosophy. Also like Rand, B. J. tended to see and communicate concepts in simple black and white terms.

B. J. was, and continues to be, a person ahead of his time. He speculated about the evolution of the species and how one of man's developing faculties is cosmic awareness. He lectured that health is the normal state of being, and when not interfered with, the innate striving of the body was usually sufficient for the regaining and maintaining of one's health.

B. J. was the living embodiment of maximizing every minute, as he often spoke about his abhorrence of goat feathers and time wasters. His motivational talks and writings consisted of rational explanations rather than esoteric rituals or authoritative commands. He was always substantive.

If you had an appointment with B. J., you had better be on time. My good friend and mentor Dr. Lyle W. Sherman, was the assistant director of the B. J. Palmer Chiropractic Research Clinic and the namesake of Sherman College of Straight Chiropractic. He worked with B. J. longer than any other chiropractor. I once asked him how B. J. was able to accomplish so much. He explained how B. J. would awake at 4 a.m. each morning, and, in good weather, he would walk in the college gardens, generally near its fountains. There he would write his notes for the day. This was before pocket voice recorders. He would then answer correspondence, often typing his own letters, perhaps give a class lecture, and write. At 11 a.m. he would enter the research clinic, expecting his patients to be ready for him to perform his spinal analysis and if necessary a vertebral adjustment. When he finished attending to his last patient, he would go to his specially made typewriter that used rolls rather than sheets of paper. He would immediately begin typing; his two index fingers would fly over the keys. When the last key was struck, he went directly to the radio/television station, WOC, which was located across the street from the campus, where he would meet with certain members of the staff. He expected them to be in his office or the conference room, prepared and waiting for him. This fast pace went on until evening. Very few things would keep B. J. up past 9 p.m. If you were visiting with him when 9 p.m. arrived, he would thank you for the visit and leave for bed.

When I was a student, he had already retired from classroom lecturing, but he occasionally would give a special morning lecture to several classes at one time in one of the smaller auditoriums. When he did this, he would stand at the entrance door looking at his big pocket watch. When the appointed time came, the door would be closed and no one dared enter.

One time, I met B. J. outside the campus' main building, and wanting to engage him in a personal conversation, I had a philosophical question ready. I went up to him and asked, "May I please have a minute with you, B. J.?" His response was one word, a dispassionate "No." Reflecting on that experience, I fully realized how B. J. took ownership of every minute of his 24 hours. I thought I would try that with my students, but could never muster the courage.

During annual Lyceum lectures, if a baby cried and was disturbing the audience, B. J. would stop his lecture and deliver one of his famous lines. Everyone knew it was coming. He would say, "Crying babies are like New Year's resolutions; they should be carried out." He would smile and the audience, and generally the parent, would laugh.

B. J. was a driven man, but he was also kind and considerate. Some second-generation chiropractors tell me that when they were children and their parent or parents were students at the Palmer School, B. J. always took time to talk to them. Dr. Sherman told me of a female patient at the research clinic who was near death, and after some cajoling, still would not cooperate in her care. One day, after B. J. gave her a good scolding, he went into his office and began to cry in empathy for her condition.

B. J. was also exceedingly generous. Tuition at the Palmer School was low because much of the income from his two radio/television stations, WOC, Davenport, and WHO, Des Moines, financially supported Palmer School. Dr. Sherman said that B. J. personally donated $180,000 a quarter, a considerable sum at the time, to the Research Clinic during the 1940s. Sherman knew B. J. also donated to the chiropractic school, but he did not know how much. One exemplary story about B. J. that has always stuck with me was that of a loyal employee at WOC who became permanently disabled. B. J. saw to it that he received his full salary for the many remaining years of his life.

B.J. stressed when people or organizations look outward to serve, they grow and flourish, and when they look inward, they atrophy. He said, "Cast your bread upon the waters, and it will return sandwiches." That witticism certainly has remained true in my life. I try to give abundantly, for giving immediately enriches my spiritual life. I am certain the act of giving also has a good effect on body chemistry. Those sandwiches have returned abundantly to me through the assistance and support of many individuals, frequently from those I have never served. I do not question how the law works, although I have some ideas. But, I have seen this law operate unfailingly in my own life and the lives of others.

Simon Senzon's categorization of the epigrams from B. J. Palmer's book, *As a Man Thinketh*, is, if not a stroke of genius, a great bounty to many. *Success, Health, and Happiness: The Epigrams of B. J. Palmer* will introduce another generation to a work that has influenced the lives of thousands over the years, and it also will change the way the epigrams are used. Rather than simply browsing, one now can access—for guidance or contemplation—all the epigrams in a particular subject area. As a result, the following pages reveal Palmer to a wider audience as one of the twentieth century's greatest minds and benefactors.

Thomas A. Gelardi

Founder, *Sherman College of Straight Chiropractic*

SUCCESS, HEALTH, AND HAPPINESS

INTRODUCTION

Success, health, and happiness were at the heart of B.J. Palmer's (1882-1961) life and teachings. Palmer's epigrams, painted everywhere on the walls of his campus embody this. The epigrams represent the wisdom, insight, and humor of one of America's greatest geniuses and luminaries from the twentieth century.

The word epigram means, "upon-written." It was developed from the epitaph, which means, "upon a tomb." Epitaphs had to be short in order to be easily carved on walls, statues, and tombs. According to Hanor Webb, "epigrams are the oldest-also the newest-forms of concise comment." Epigrams can be funny, wise (as in proverbs or aphorisms or sayings), reverent or irreverent, simple or subtle.[1] There are few rules for what actually comprises an epigram. In modern times, epigrams are thought to have wit. Samuel Taylor Coleridge wrote,

What is an epigram? A dwarfish whole,

Its body brevity, and wit its soul.

The wit is often taken to be a sting at the end. William Walsh wrote,

An epigram should be – if right-

Short, simple, pointed, keen, and bright,

A lively little thing!

Like wasp with taper body – bound

By lines – not many, neat and round,

All ending in a sting.

Some epigrams are beautiful, elated, and honoring (without a sting). In Paul Nixon's classic book on the modern epigram, he concluded it may be solemn or savage, a love poem, or an elegy, amusing, moral, or philosophical. So long as it is brief, with some, "graceful, ingenious, pointed, weighty, witty, or satirical turn of thought to which it's preceding lines lead up."[2]

Palmer's use of epigrams can be traced to two of his early mentors, his father and Elbert Hubbard. One of the oldest books in his father D.D. Palmer's collection was titled, *The Moral Aphorisms and Terseological Teachings of Confucius: The Sapient Chinese Philosopher*.[3] B.J. started using epigrams to advertise by modeling Hubbard, founder of Roycrofters, an artist community in New York. Hubbard had a strong influence on B.J. in thought, dress, politics, and business. B.J. actually modeled his "prettiest printing plant in America" on Hubbard's.[4] Purple epigrams were painted on the walls of the Printery alongside the green plants and singing birds.[5] Later he modified some of Hubbard's epigrams and borrowed freely from others.[6,7] Palmer also included attributed epigrams liberally. Over 100 epigrams by other authors are reproduced in this volume. Palmer's epigrams from his book, *As a Man Thinketh*,[8] total 1,059 although the Palmer Campus reports there were close to 3,000 epigrams on the walls of all the buildings.[9]

As a Man Thinketh was originally published around 1921 and was 73 pages. The page numbers increased in each of five editions until the 1930s edition, where there were 129 pages. That edition was reproduced in 1952 as a chapter in Palmer's book, *Answers*, and in 1988 by the Delta Sigma Chi Fraternity.[10] I will make an educated guess that there was an addition of about 730 epigrams from 1920s to the 1930s. Considering Palmer's process for writing an epigram, "Give Us 30 Days and We'll Write a Book; 6 Months and We'll Write a Chapter; 1 Year and We'll Write an Epigram,"[11] writing 730 in about 20 years is tremendous!

According to one of Palmer's deans, Herbert Hender, *As A Man Thinketh* was written down because people were constantly copying the epigrams. Hender wrote, "Hundreds everywhere. B.J. believes in making bare walls work. Many people go about copying them in note books. In self-defense, he printed them in a book titled *As A Man Thinketh.*"[12] Publishing the epigrams for profit was consistent with Palmer's entrepreneurial spirit. He wrote two successful books on advertising.[13]

Palmer's influence extended beyond his students and faculty. Napoleon Hill was a great proponent of affirmations and aphorisms, and one of the pioneers of success thinking in the last century. On his meeting with Palmer in the 1920s he wrote, "Here I found the most inspiring institution of any kind--bar none!--in America. Here I found MY teacher! A man who not only teaches about things, but how to do things. A man who embodies in his life and work the principles of living and doing, the fine "Art of selling Yourself. . . ."[14] Hill was clearly inspired by Palmer.

Many of B.J.'s speeches such as "Selling Yourself" were "epigrams expanded upon."[15] From chiropractic's unique style of advertising to Palmer's charismatic approach to getting the message across, epigrams became a simple way to share his message.[16]

In the chapter following his 1952 reproduction of the epigrams, Palmer wrote,

Our endeavor in making idle, non-productive space work, was to explain the secrets and mysteries of how to get sick well; the same as it is our endeavor to make blank, bare walls of our buildings work, with epigrams which speak a language of action and a philosophy of life.[17]

At the core of these epigrams are kernels of truth, aspects of humanity, inspiration to strive to be better, to evolve, and to grow. Palmer used them to inspire his students and faculty to excel. In his introduction to the epigrams he wrote, "See it and you read it; read it and you think it; think it and it becomes you; becoming you, you are it – thus we build better, bigger, broader men and women."[18] The wider vision to create the book of epigrams was so the message, "may spread beyond those only who see." Thus it is not only for those walking the hallowed halls, or chiropractors and their patients, but for all. Epigrams continue to play a role as an inspiration for the chiropractic profession,[19] but these words put together by Palmer are desugned to inspire anyone who seeks to be more, to step up, and to challenge themselves to follow their inner prompting to grow, to get closer to the divine, and to take decisive action.

The only problem with the original editions of these epigrams was that they were not organized. Gaining the wisdom from them was always hit or miss. An attempt to make them easier to access was made years ago in the form of an index but it relied on historical organization.[20] This edition is organized by topic. Each section is categorized according to general themes such as success, hard times, common sense, business, and wisdom. It is my hope that this organization will facilitate great insight and enlightenment for all who read them.

I have written introductions based on the theme of each chapter. The introductions are very brief and are designed to give you, the reader, a richer understanding of Palmer's perspective. Since the epigrams are generally from the 1920s and 1930s, I have included quotes from Palmer's later writings in the 1950s. This will help you to understand how Palmer developed and place the epigrams in a wider and deeper context.

The epilogue is a new essay, *B.J. Palmer: An Integral Biography*. It explores Palmer's life and the levels of consciousness he may have developed to. The article is based on an earlier epilogue from my first book, *The Spiritual Writings of B.J. Palmer*.[20] This incarnation of the essay has been through extensive peer-review for the *Journal of Integral Theory and Practice*.[21] There are some small changes from the article so it fits the book. The epilogue is an in-depth approach to examining Palmer's interior development and legacy.

Finally, BJ once wrote, "One of my epigrams is this—and ponder it well, "WHAT THE FELLOW IS, INSIDE, IS! WHAT THE FELLOW IS, INSIDE, WILL COME OUT SOONER OR LATER!"[22] May these epigrams assist you as they have thousands before you to come out soon from within and let shine the glorious essence you truly are.

1. God and Innate

Bartlett Joshua Palmer's perspective on God was unique. He viewed God as a part of everything, deeply intertwined as the intelligence, the wisdom, and the substance of all matter. For living matter, such as human beings, he acknowledged an even deeper reality, that Innate Intelligence or just Innate for short was the soul of the universe. By getting in touch with your own Innate, you could get in touch with God directly. For most people however, this process was interfered with by their Educated Intelligence or just Educated for short. When Educated attempts to run everything and know everything, Innate is not easily heard. When Innate is listened to and heeded, life unfolds, success emerges, and health and happiness are at hand. The key to listening to that "Wee sma' voice," is to pay attention to "thot flashes," and receive chiropractic adjustments to allow Innate to be expressed through your own body more fully.

These realizations developed in Palmer over the course of 60 years. The earliest expression of these ideas came from his father, D.D. Palmer, who developed them from the teachings of Spiritualism and magnetic healing. The real uniqueness was B.J.'s deepening wisdom and clarity of connection to Innate. He learned to listen to Innate and act on its' promptings. This ability helped him to develop in his material success and his spirituality.

In his final years of life, B.J. Palmer even referred to himself as "We" in order to include Innate and Educated speaking with one voice. In this use of "We" he included all people working towards the developing worldview centered on Innate. In its highest expression, the voice of "We" was the voice of the One speaking through the many. Palmer wrote, "Innate communicates with you and when Innate is in contact you are in tune with the infinite."[1] In his later years, Palmer began to write about being in touch with Innate as a form of enlightenment all people have access to. He wrote,

"Yet INSIDE HIM is that greater INSIDE world he does not know, seldom recognizes, never fully understands. His limited finite understanding seeks to know the infinite unlimited world surrounding him, but fails dismally to realize that world he seeks is WITHIN HIM. Should that time come when his finite mind could and did KNOW the infinite mind WITHIN, then his external finite mind would cease to be, because it would then be infinite in scope, understanding, and application."[2]

We believe that God is here, and that we are as near Him now as ever shall be. We do not believe that He started this world a-going and went away and left it to run itself.

———

Feel glum? Keep mum. Want to grumble? Be humble. Trials cling? Just sing. Can't sing? Just cling. Feel fear? God's near. Money goes? He knows. Honor left? Not bereft. Is there rust? Work! Trust.

———

We are coming to think of God as dwelling in man, rather than as operating on man from without.

———

God gave us man and woman. No greater function can man perform in thanks to God than the conservation of man, for man, in behalf of man, for God

———

Cleanliness is Godliness. Is the champeen long-distance, corner-hitter, tobacco-spitter a God?

———

Prayer Is Affirmation to Education to Bolster Education's Theories of God.

———

People who set themselves up as authorities about God are prisoners in primitive concepts. Their educations are confined in dungeons of obsolete-fear-theology.

———

God divided Man into men that they might help each other.

Many People Instruct God What to Do, How, When, Where, and Why. Take Orders and Report for Duty.

———

"Serving God" Is Doing Good to Man; Praying Is Thought to Be an Easier "Service," therefore Is More Generally Chosen.

—Benjamin Franklin

———

God is an urge!
Mortals would do better if they knew how.

———

Robert Browning said: "God's in His Heaven. All's right with the world."

———

Faith is the ability to believe what we do not see.
The reward of faith is to see what we did not believe.

———

Most men forget God all day and ask Him to remember them at night.

———

Miracles are manifestations for which science has no definition, no analysis.

———

We are only one, but we are one;
We can do some things.
What we can do, we shall do.
With Innate, we WILL.

Man Does not Contact God. God Contacts Man.

Man Does not Contact Innate. Innate Contacts Man.

God Contacts Innate, Innate Contacts Educated.

All that Is Good, Worth While, Permanent, Comes from

Above Down; Inside Out.

That Is THE Law.

Religions Reverse the Law.

———

You Can Deceive Others Easily; Yourself, Perhaps, for a Time; but Innate, Never.

———

Many Men Are More Sure of the Devil than of Divinity.

—Cope

———

You Have two Chances—

One of Getting the Germ and One of not.

And if You Get the Germ

You have two Chances—

One of Getting the Disease and One of not.

And if You Get the Disease

You Have two Chances—

One of Dying and One of not.

And if You Die—

You Will still Have two Chances

———

Man Is Sub-natural; therefore Things Natural Are Rated "SUPERnatural."

Innate Being with Us, Who Can Be against Us? We Welcome Responsibilities, Crave Difficult Work, Seek Dangerous Duty. These Are Divine Opportunities for Service and Growth.

———

Men Who Accomplish Much Work in Harmony with Natural Laws—They Permitted the Divine to Express Itself thru Them.

———

Innate's purpose in using us is to spend forces for something which outlasts today.

———

One reason we run deliriously and noisily about empty living is because we do not know how to reach Innate, and that admission is terrible for us to face.

———

We experience disruption on the surface of human behavior to know what has been invisibly developed within Innate may come into being.

———

Innate is the Soul of the Universe concealed and revealed in an animal.

———

2. Hard Times

B.J. Palmer was certainly familiar with hard times. It was during his greatest challenges that he learned to thrive. From his early days as a street-kid in Davenport, Iowa, being raised by a series of step mothers, being expelled from high-school to taking over the fledgling school of chiropractic from his father at age twenty, he knew hard times. Of his earliest years, Palmer wrote, in his book, *Fight to Climb*,

It truly is a Horatio Alger story...

The Palmer family—five of us—moved from Burlington, Iowa, to Davenport, when we were four years old. Father was so engrossed in his work that he practically left the bringing up...of us three kids to his wife, who was our fourth stepmother. We roamed streets and alleys. We were alley cats, wharf-rats, dead-end kids. We knew every alley in downtown district, every back stairs into every building, every hiding place, every place where drygoods boxes were piled. We knew every garbage can and every grocery store refuse pile where we could find best pickings of choice pieces of food too bad to sell, but good enough for us to eat.[1]

In each early challenge he responded by adapting, changing, growing, and thriving. After his father left Davenport in 1902, leaving him the school and the practice to run, B.J. secured a loan and took out a full-page ad in the local paper. Faced with jail in 1903 for practicing medicine without a license, Palmer secured a loan and expanded the student body of his school. Challenged by the medical establishment and the newly licensed osteopathic profession, Palmer forced the issue in 1907, went to court and became a professional witness in hundreds (if not thousands) of the trials of chiropractors, winning most of them. In at least two instances of revolt from his faculty due to his leadership and direction, first in 1909 and then again in 1924, Palmer stuck to his principles and continued to develop his profession. When the stock market crashed in 1929 and their bank accounts were wiped out, Palmer focused on his fledgling radio station, whose revenues rescued the school and allowed him to open a million dollar research clinic in the 1930s. In these quotes about hard times, he speaks from direct experience. Palmer was clearly one of the founders of the self-help movement in America as he set the example, lived the success, and wrote down his keys for us to prosper from.

When you get to the end of your rope, tie a knot in it and hang on.

———

He who laughs last is some lifter.

———

He who enters here gets all he has coming.

———

Make Light of Troubles and Gloom of Misfortune Will Vanish.

———

There are no hard times coming. It's just soft times going.

———

Do Reverses Trouble You? A Worm Is the Only Thing That Can't Fall Down.

———

The only people who enjoy hearing your troubles are lawyers who make money patching 'em up; doctors who get paid for ripping 'em out; and preachers who accept gratuities for praying 'em away.

———

A horse must be "broke" before he will work. Just so with some men.

———

About the time you think you make both ends meet, somebody moves the ends.

———

Even a tombstone will say good things about a fellow when he's down.

B.J.P.—one who has both succeeded and failed; but one who has succeeded in spite of his failures.

———

Great pilots are made in rough waters and in deep seas.

"Boost and the world boosts with you;"
Knock and you're on the shelf;
For the world gets sick of one who kicks
And wishes he'd kick himself.

———

We would rather be a has-been than a never-was, Because a never-was never was, and a has-been has been.

———

We know many "hard knocks" graduates who are educated, who cannot write their names. They are illiterate but not ignorant.

———

The failure says: "They wouldn't give me a show." Nobody gave Barnum a show, but he had the biggest on earth.

———

Most advantages are generally disadvantages.

———

Spell "now" backwards and you have the answer.

———

When we hear people say, "I hope the time may speedily come when I shall have no more obstacles," we feel like adding, "When that time comes, ring up the undertaker, for you'll be a dead one."

———

When You Get into a Tight Place and Everything Goes Against You until It Seems You Cannot Hold on, Hold on then, for that Is Just the Place and Time the Tide Will Turn.

—Harriet Beecher Stowe

First the sneer, then the cheer; the lash, then the laurel; the curse, then the caress; the trial, then the triumph; the cross, then the crown.

———

It doesn't behoove any of us to live too much on our "dignity," because 98% of us are accidents.

———

The harder you hit a straight nail the sooner it arrives. The harder you hit a crooked one the sooner it bends and buckles.

———

The war has crushed the juice out of the orange on the tree of life and nothing is left but the peel over which materialism is slipping to its doom.

———

We will come out all right in the end—Jonah did.

———

Life's tests reveal character. Winter reveals the pine as an evergreen.

———

What's wrong WITH ME!

———

How much pain have cost us the evils that never happened.

———

What is hard, isn't fun.
What is fun, isn't hard.

———

Somebody has said that one-half the world is sinning and the other half is weeping over the sins of the first half.

—Dr. Charles Milton Newcomb,
Psychologist, Author, and Humorist

It Isn't the Size of the Dog in a Fight, but the Size of the Fight in the Dog.

———

Any Coward Can Fight a Battle When He's Winning, but Give Me a Man Who Has Pluck to Fight When He Is Losing.

———

In Adversity It Is Easy to Despise Life; Brave Man Is He Who Can Endure and Be Miserable.

———

Shortest Cut to "Heaven" Is Lifting One out of "Hell."

———

Little Minds Are Tamed and Subdued by Misfortune: Great Minds Rise Above Them.   —Washington Irving

———

If You Win the Race, "It Was Fair;" If You Lose, "You Were Pocketed."

———

What Appear to Be Calamities Are often the Sources of Fortune
                                        —Beaconsfield

———

Life Is a See-Saw. Be Decent to Man Who Is Down—He May Be Up Tomorrow.   —Huebner

———

Little Minds Are Wounded by Little Things; Great Minds See All and Are not Hurt.   —DeRochefocauld

———

A Neurotic Is One with Both Feet Firmly Planted in Mid Air.

The Great Flood Was Sent because of so Many Dirty People.

———

I Had No Shoes and Complained until I Met a Man who Had no Feet.   —Arabian Proverb

———

An Optimist Sees an Opportunity in Every Calamity. A Pessimist Sees a Calamity in Every Opportunity.

———

For Every Man Who Fails because of Inability, There Are a Hundred Who Fail because They Lack Power to Stick.

———

Trouble is Fire in which Character Is Tried.

———

It Is Easy to Find Fault if one Has That Disposition. There Was once a Man Who, Unable to Find Fault with His Goal, Complained There Were too Many Prehistoric Toads in It.   —Mark Twain

———

No Man Knoweth Light Until he Sits in the Shadow.

———

Pessimist Stands Beneath Tree of Prosperity and Growls when the Fruit Falls on His Head.

———

A Man Who Bounces Up when Hs Is Knocked Down Is of Use.

———

Work of Man Is to Fight against Difficulties which His Activities Have Stirred up.   —Burggraeve

A Certain Amount of Fleas Is Good for a Dog—Keeps Him from Broodin' on Bein' a Dog.

—David Harum

———

Success Is Measured by What a Man Accomplishes, by Opposition He Encountered and Courage He Maintained in Struggle Against Odds.

———

It's Easy Enough to Be Happy
When Life Rolls Along Like a Song,
But the Man That's Worth While
Is the Man That Will Smile
When Everything Goes Dead Wrong.   —Wilcox

———

Better a scar to show the arrow came
Than to go thru life unscathed by any mark;
Better the ashes eloquent of flame
Than have the spirit's heart, forever dark;
Better to lose than miss the chance of gain
Better a broken than a rusted knife!
Better to love, even as a pain,
Than meeting death, all unaware of life.   —Elinor Lennen

———

The cynic knows the price of everything and the value of nothing.

———

Opposing Circumstances Create Strength and Stiffen Backbone. "Bucking the Line" Is Better.

Best Education Is Obtained by Struggling to Make a Living. What Is Defeat? A Stepping Stone to Something Better.   —Wendell Phillips

———

Why Damn the Fellow Who Hands You a Lemon? You Can Make Lemonade.

———

Some Folks Have more Temptations than Others because They Hunt for Them.

———

When we are right, no one remembers. When we are wrong, no one forgets.

———

Once, men were the reason for everything; now they appear to be least important quantity.

———

If You Refuse to Face Facts, They Become Terrors, Nightmares, Horrors.

———

As a Game of Cards, so Is Life; We Must Play What Is Dealt. Glory Consists Much in Winning and in Playing a Poor Hand Well.

—Josh Billings

———

Hail the Storm. It Is your Antagonist Come to Develop You.

———

Persistent People Begin Success Where Others End in Failure.

———

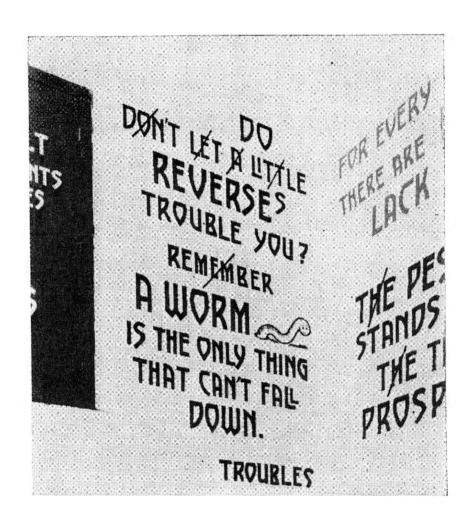

3. Action

B.J. Palmer was a master at taking action. His accomplishments are many, from being an expert chiropractor, a technique developer, a publisher, author, teacher, a school administrator, professional leader, world traveler, organist, entrepreneur, radio and television pioneer, the list goes on. Palmer wrote,

> Some men are large enuf to become mayors, others governors, some presidents. Some men have opened one door only, others open many doors and develop many talents such as thinkers, writers, printers, cafeteria, radio stations, authors, lecturers, builders, philosophers, A Little Bit O' Heaven, Clinic Gardens, growth of roses, orchids, ad infinitum. How can one man do so much when he *educationally* knows so little? It's easy when Innate points the way. Innate opens one or more doors of un*limited* wisdom, flows *thru* to education; education *accepts* without hesitation, acts and moves, and all comes out the big *end* of the horn of success. It's hard, difficult and impossible when education *scoffs* at Innate, *refuses* to receive and accept what Innate offers, and thus we again account for failures in our ranks and those of other professions.[1]

One of Palmer's keys to success was to act on his intuitive hunches from Innate, his "thot flashes" (BJ often preferred a shortened spelling of thought to save space). The principle he developed based on this technique is easy to follow; pay attention to the little hints of direction, action, and purpose Innate is constantly whispering to you. Act on it immediately. When success follows and it surely will, act again and again and again on every whisper. After a while, Educated will be sublimated to the superconscious Innate. You will find yourself taking action out of habit and conviction, depth of soul, and depth of heart. Palmer wrote,

> The value TO mankind of that "God"-LAW IN man depends upon how well man permits that "God"-law IN man to express itself, and how much he utilizes that LAW OF LIFE to become A LAW OF EVERY DAY ACTION in himself AND IN OTHERS, wherein he aims to liberate THAT LAW in himself as well as in others.
>
> Time ALWAYS has and ALWAYS WILL perpetuate those methods which better serve mankind.[2]

You must act upon them now. It is through action that divine purpose takes place in the world. Through action, the world is co-created because Innate can then fulfill its expression through you and as you.

Nearest explanation one can give is: when *education* reaches that degree of exalted understanding that it recognizes there IS an Innate, knows WHAT Innate IS, grasps importance of bigness of that Innate personality; then *Innate* becomes aware that education IS READY to be directed by it. Innate will then COME TO EDUCATION with thot flashes in exact frequency of degree of understanding, recognition, and importance education relies upon Innate. When thot flashes arrive

FROM Innate TO education, education *must* rely upon them, *act* upon them, not tomorrow but now, and not question them. HOW is one to recognize difference between educated ideas and Innate's thots? Answer is clear: When you KNOW what Innate is, Innate will so *vividly* impress its thots upon education that you WILL recognize difference between dullness of one and brilliancy of other. But, beware! If Innate flashes a thot and you educationally debate, argue, hesitate, question its accuracy, quality, value, or correctness, Innate will retire and forget your needs and necessities and withdraw until you ARE ready, at some future time, if at all.[3]

SOW WITH HARVEST IN MIND

We can't beat the law of cause and effect. What goes into the past has got to come out of the future. What we sow we must eventually reap.

But we can start today to plant seeds of a better life for ourselves.

We can never hope to know all laws, nor can we understand all mysteries which govern both body and mind.

But we can understand enough to be, to a very great extent, "masters of our fate."

I am convinced by replacing negative, destructive and unwholesome thoughts with constructive, courageous and helpful thoughts, we can improve our health, relationships with others and chances for success and happiness. Control of mind is very often control of causes.

Let us open our minds and discipline our thoughts and actions, that we may better understand God's laws and become more efficient workers and "masters of our fate."[4]

Life's rich rewards go to doers, not to promisers.

———

Energy is the capital, God-given, for the great game of life.

———

We know there is something doing, somewhere, for every man ready to do it. We know we're ready—right now!

———

Think!

———

We should live in an age of "Thou Shalt!"
Nine of the ten Commandments are written "Thou Shalt NOT!"

———

It is the tragedy of progress that you have got to make good or make room.

———

With ourself, by ourself, we must go on, and on, and on, and that's just what we are going to do. Aren't you?

———

We want to go thru life admitting truth, facing facts; taking lickings like a man, winning calmly, and, above all, not being a piker.

———

Don't go among the doers, if you don't want to be did.

———

A hen does not quit scratching just because the worms are scarce. She scratches that much more to make her living.

Throw away your wishbone, straighten up your backbone, stick out your jawbone and go to it.

———

"Everything comes to him who waits"—
But, here is one that's slicker:
The man who goes after what he wants,
Gets it a darn sight quicker.

———

"Heads up!" Shoulders erect, Face front, "Forward march!"

———

The greatest pleasure we know is to do a good action by stealth and to have it found out by accident.

———

THINK! SPEAK! ACT, POSITIVES!
I AM!
I WILL!
I CAN!
I MUST!

———

Don't take things as they come—head 'em off.

———

The crime of the hour is the lack of physical production and mental cooperation.

———

"I wish I was a rock, a-settin' on a hill, a-doin' nothing all day long, but jest a settin' still. I wouldn't eat; I wouldn't sleep; I wouldn't even wash. I'd jest set still a thousand years, and rest myself, by-gosh."

The magnetism all original action exerts is explained when we inquire the reason of self-trust.

———

The fact that we are not buried is no proof we are alive.

———

We must get ready to get.

———

Words Are Cheap. Deeds Are Priceless.

———

"Leave well enough alone" and you'll stay on the bottom.

———

Do we feel more shame for what we have done, or for what the world has found out that we have done?

———

The efficient man works through a philosophy, which is a state of mind rather than a plan, system, or method.

———

The less you do the more probable it is right. The more you do the more probable it is wrong.

———

Harder our hitters hit, faster the quitters quit.

———

The most important thing that Columbus ever did was to start.

———

IN-Action is the seed of content—INACTION is the seed of discontent.

The only time for cherry pie is when cherries are ripe. Why wait?

———

The soul occupied with great ideas, best performs small duties.

———

Not only strike while the iron is hot, but make it hot by striking.

———

If you intend to be happy don't be foolish enuf to wait for a just cause.

———

Life only avails, not the having lived.

———

The time you lose has the same potential value as the time you use.

———

Some men never hit the mark because they never pull the trigger.

———

Do and the world does with you. Don't and you do alone.

———

What if they do say! And, what if they mean it! It's what YOU do that counts.

———

"If you're a self-starter the boss won't have to be a crank."

———

Make the do-so just a little better than the say-so.

———

Some people expect to attain success like a person taking a train; by taking a seat and waiting for the conductor to call the station.

———

Weak men wait for opportunities; strong men make them.

WAIT and your ship will be a RECEIVER ship.

———

There are no sleeping cars on the Success Road.

———

Human Race is Divided into Two Classes: Those Who Do Something, and Those Who Sit and Ask, Let's Do It the Other Way?

—Holmes

———

Let us paraphrase one of America's greatest psychologists when he practically said: "When you don't feel the way you ought to act if you just act the way you ought to feel, then you will feel the way you ought to act." William James meant this: "When you don't feel the way you ought to act, if you will act the way you ought to feel, then you will feel the way you ought to act."

—Major Thornton Anthony Mills,
Lecturer, Member Air Corps Res. U.S. Army

———

Most Things that Are Put Off till Tomorrow Should Have Been Done Yesterday.

———

There's Quite a Difference between Itching for It, and Scratching for It.

———

Valuable Men Are Recognized by Deeds and Products, not by Boasts.

———

Pre-meditation Is 9/10ths Past-Accomplishment. Pre-meditation Side-tracks 9 of 10 Mistakes.

Some People Forget a Ship Can Only Come in After It Has Been Sent Out.

―――――

The Only Way to Save Seed Is to Sow It.

―――――

When in Doubt, Don't!
When Convinced, Act!

―――――

If the universe is a universe of thought, its creation must have been actions of thought.

―――――

TAKIN' BEATS TALKIN'.

―――――

There Are Two Reasons for Doing Anything—a Good Reason and the Real Reason.

―――――

Symptoms of laziness and fatigue are identical.

―――――

Work Is What Other People Have for You to Do. Play Is What You Think of Yourself.

―――――

Use Your Eyes Before Your Feet When You Cross the Street.

―――――

It is not how long one lives; it is how much. The tortoise lives long, but not much. The bee lives much, but not long.

―――――

It Is Impossible to Be Right when the Reason for Action Is Wrong.

Use is positive, active, life-giving. Use is alive. Use adds to the sum total.

———

Build strong!

———

The World Is not much Interested in the Storms You Encountered at Sea.

Question is: Did You Bring the Ship into Port?

———

Work, today, as tho we were going to live always. Live, today, as tho you were going to die tonight.

———

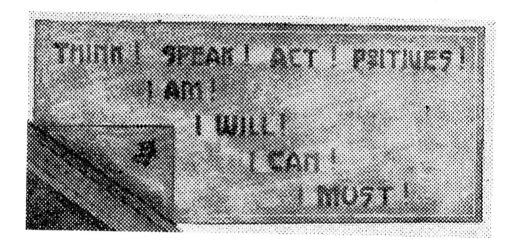

4. Abundance and Success

B.J. Palmer embodied success and abundance. His mansion on the hill was filled with antiques and relics from around the world. His many collections included Buddha statues, osteological specimens, vases, blades, phallus statues, knives, and circus paraphernalia. At the core of his success was his firm belief that by allowing Innate to flow and act its natural course, all would unfold as it should. He wrote,

"There's always a ladder and room at top if one wants to climb hard enough, strong enough, and long enough. There's always an Innate to push if you're willing to permit yourself to *be* pushed. There's always a goal if one *has* vision. There's always an objective if one *remains true* to an honest and sincere conviction. There's always attainment possible if one remains steadfast to a correct principle and practice."[1]

Palmer wrote extensively on genius and sincerely believed that those who were successful in the past were so because of their ability to access the storehouse of unlimited resources within. He developed his philosophy from direct experience. In his earliest years, Palmer learned to tap his inner potential and couple it to positive thinking. Add to this his incredible persistence and success was assured. He wrote,

Peculiarly, this boy began to rely MORE AND MORE upon Innate thot-flashes and less on educated opinions of those who surrounded him. They sincerely and honestly advised him NOT to do this THAT way, but preferably he should do what THEY WANTED him to do some educated way which his executives and advisors thot was better. More and more, he followed advices of Innate. Eventually, he was able to get many helpmates to ALSO see Innate's ways had paid big dividends in HIS success; therefore they began to listen to THEIR Innates and they, too, came thru as followers of Innate's processes.[2]

If you want to be Rich, Give!

If you want to be Poor, Grasp!

If you want to be Abundance, Scatter!

If you want to be Needy, Hoard!

———

Being Yourself

———

To win GRIN—To fail WAIL.

———

We believe in courtesy, in kindness, in generosity, in good cheer, in friendship and in honest competition.

———

You'll get further by out-thinking a prospect than you will by trying to out-talk him.

———

Say nothing when you have nothing to say, and keep on saying nothing when the prospect has something to say.

———

Altruism is an essential to success.

———

For years we have been watching big business men and we have found few men of spectacular talents among them. They have three well-balanced qualities: To observe to reflect, and to apply.

———

Man is dust! Dust settles! Be a man!

———

Men of principle are the principal men.

Why tell unfriendly critics to go to the deuce? Think it—and go on with your rat-killing.

———

As we change size, we automatically change our place. No matter what place we have shaken into, if we get smaller, we'll rattle down to a smaller place. If we get bigger, we'll shake up to a bigger place.

———

There are more great places than small places begging for people big enough to fill them.

———

It's grow or go!

———

Where there's a way, there's a will.

———

Be a live wire and you won't be stepped on!

———

Most people vegetate like turnips. They let the sun and rain work their will. Perhaps this is no crime. Indeed, it may be the great human destiny. But, it is not the way to the top of the ladder.

———

We have been in business some years. We started at the bottom. We are rapidly climbing. We are above many, below some others. We have been cussed, discussed, boycotted, talked about, lied about, and lied against, damned, browbeaten, tried for murder, whipsawed, stood up and knocked down. The only reason we are in business now, is to see what in hell is going to happen next!

Rule No. 9: Don't take yourself too damned seriously.

————

Fletcherize!

————

Success consists in the climb.

————

By Outward Acts we judge Inward Thots.

————

The world makes a path for the man who knows where he is going.

————

The world bestows its big prizes, both in money and honors, for but one thing, and that is initiative. It is doing the right thing without being told. But next to doing the thing without being told is to do it right when told once.

————

Failure is only for those who think failure.

————

We believe in working diligently and earnestly, laughing heartily— and loving everybody and everything sincerely.

————

Success or failure remains with you; no one will push you any way but out, unless you do your share of the work.

————

Youth is curious, and success is a game for curiosity seekers. Stay young!

————

The Formula for Failure Is: Try to Please Everybody.

The doughboys won victories on the firing line. You can win others on the dotted line.

―――――

No man or woman succeeds who does not, knowingly or unwittingly, obey law.

―――――

Keeping everlastingly at it brings success—and nervous breakdowns. The element of success is intelligent idleness.

―――――

When you and we quit taking ourselves seriously and realize we are workers in a great shop, rebuilding humans; where every hump, failure and disappointment is just an experiment that didn't work; and go on trying to hit the one that will work, we'll find the secret of success and happiness.

―――――

It is easy to convince the loser that it is wrong to gamble.

―――――

The criminal of this day is he who produces the vacant hour. The success always produces the crowded hour.

―――――

A certain requisite in making a success is the ability to look a fact in the face without blinking and to know a fact when you see it.

―――――

I'm Proof Against "Failure;" I've Seen Behind It. Only Failure a Man Ought to Fear Is Failure in Cleaving to the Purpose He Sees Is Best.

—George Elliot

What is owning all the world to a man if his wife is a widow?

————

When we look back on human history we shall find many men who were considered failures when they died and are regarded as successes now.

————

The man who exchanges character for cash; purity for power; principle for party; manhood for money; soul for silver; God for gold, is a failure.

————

When you get to making big money, keep your small feet on terra firma.

————

It is all right to spend money to make character; it is all wrong to spend character to make money.

————

You may give until you are rich,
And keep until you are poor.

————

Success is not made by lying awake at night, but in keeping awake in the daytime.

————

The best way to get ahead and stay ahead is to use your head.

————

A fellow never appreciates being up and out until he is down and in.

————

Ambition is the years that make the thoro-bred.

Happiness is easily secured. What fearful prices some men pay for imitations.

―――――

"Tho days be dark and trade be tough, it's always well to make a bluff, to face the world with cheerful eye, as tho the goose were hanging high."

―――――

The boot-black makes his success by standing at the foot while aiming at the top.

―――――

Use All You Need. Need All You Use.

―――――

Love of Money Is Root of All Evil. Most Men Are Willing to Eat Dirt While Digging for the Root.   —Speed

―――――

A Fellow May Have more Money than Brains, but not Long.

―――――

Trouble with being a good sport is you have to lose to prove it.

―――――

It is not by a man's purse, but by his character, that he is rich or poor.

―――――

What everybody can have, nobody wants; but what only one person can have, there's a queue to get.

―――――

Money Is a Means not an End. Twist It and the End Becomes Mean.

―――――

Is It a Sin to Have Possessions? It IS a Sin when Possessions Have Us.

THE LADDER OF SUCCESS

100%—I did.

90%—I will.

80%—I can.

70%—I think I can.

60%—I might.

50%—I think I might.

40%—What is it?

30%—I wish I could.

20%—I don't know how.

10%—I can't.

0%—I won't.

———

Our Reward Is in the Race We Run, not in the Prize.

—Rogers

———

Success depends upon desire backed by will, expressed in intelligent and persistent action.

———

26. In the home of author. Living Room. Largest Japanese
cloisonne vase in the world. Compare size.

---

5. Genius

Palmer firmly believed that his ability to tap into his own genius was directly linked to his ability to listen to Innate. If this was so for him, such must it be for all, because every person has access to Innate. In this quote, he is responding to a book by the religious scholar, Marcus Bach, who wrote of the enlightened spiritual teachings of various individuals throughout the world. Palmer wrote,

> "Genius" is not secret of a few. It is buried in all. You write about those who have dug deep, dug up, and put on exhibition what "genius" is. But what is more important is to arouse that same genius that is up-high buried in ALL people. If this were not so, they would be dead and buried, for THEY do represent THE genius that built them, runs them every day they live. To recognize IT, let IT shine thru the dense dark deep jungles of too much superficial education, should be the work of those who HAVE FOUND THEMSELVES.[1]

Palmer later expanded on this notion of genius. It comes from above, somehow into the brain, down through the body via the spinal cord. This flow of energy and health through the body is the same source as the flow of genius from the infinite spring of wisdom and knowledge informing all matter, all life, through all time.

"Genius" as we dub it, is nothing more or less than the individual who listens, accepts without question and permits development of a superior knowledge FROM WITHIN to flow freely WITHOUT questioning that which flows freely from ABOVE-DOWN WITHIN-OUT—That's why genius IS genius. He has learned to respect those subterranean thot-flashes thereby keeping pathways open and receptive. If he wakes in the night with "an idea," he captures it then and there, doing the thing, whatever it is, when it is coming. Most would roll over and go back to sleep and forget it. Genius IS genius because they have and utilize that peculiar faculty of absorbing from a source greater than they know, the inherent capacities of receiving and using those "inspirations, aspirations and perspirations" that come so freely from within out, refusing to reject them from within-out.[2]

Unfortunate is he who is born a genius. Nobody will believe him while he is alive. And everybody is jealous of him until he dies.

———

Many a man has the eyesight of a hawk and the vision of a clam.

———

The world loves a living negative, but honors its dead positives.
It likewise fights its living positives and forgets its dead negatives.

———

Thinking is more difficult than the rowing of a boat against a sea; harder than the digging of coal; requiring greater strength and skill than wielding broadswords; requiring more grit than facing winter winds; so difficult it is to think down to the core of things and to solve problems as yet unknown and still unraveled.

———

Awaken the germs of genius in man and he will do something worthwhile.

———

True ideas are those we can assimilate, validate, corroborate and verify.

———

They copied all they could follow, but they couldn't follow our mind; and we left them sweating and stealing, ten years and a half behind.

———

Familiar as the voice of the mind is to each, the highest merit we ascribe to Moses, Plato and Milton is that they set at naught books and traditions, and spoke not what men, but what they thought.

———

Get the idea—all else follows.

You dead and buried ideas of yesterday, let go! Let go!

———

The average individual IS average.

———

There is a power within—a fountain head of unlimited resource — and he who controls it controls circumstances instead of it controlling him.

———

The gods take care not to mix even a drop of pedantry in the makeup of the rare men whom they destine for great deeds.

———

Nothing is waste that touches the man of genius.

———

He is a man who has merely the ordinary qualities that he shares with his fellows; but who has developed those ordinary qualities to a more than ordinary degree.

———

Universities are, of course, hostile to geniuses, who seeing and using ways of their own, discredit routine and books, as schools and colleges persecute and crush individuality.

———

In the justical world all the elements, forces, and combinations act and develop together as one manifestation at one time. Mental analysis but unites them stronger.

———

We appreciate the power of being able to be useful to mankind.

Many a man who disappears under a cloud is discovered later to have provided a silver lining for that same cloud.

————

When a man turns from his visions, he lies.

————

A new idea is like exercise—It makes you sore at first. But later on the system gets used to it.

—Bernie Schultz.

————

Vision

To see what others do not see.

To see further than others.

To see before they do.

————

It's pretty hard for the average man to realize that constantly the IDEALISTIC is defeating the REALISTIC.

————

We rejoice in the power to be a channel for the expression of the divine purpose.

————

Every single thing is related to every other thing, and illuminated minds are the periods that separate the cycles. The law remains fixed.

————

Genius is elemental. It influences humanity as much as heat and cold, rain and sunshine. People who suffer the greatest opposition to it are those who fall before its onward march. Others get in step.

Great men float into power on mystical waves moved by the force of destiny. The greater the mind the greater the fixtures of force behind it.

———

The higher intelligence needs less control but more development; from within rather than from without.

———

Destiny is the collective conscience acting through elective genius.

———

Imagination does not do everything, but you can't do anything without it.   —William Rainey Bennett, Lecturer, Philosopher, and Humorist

———

You talk about the dreamer, but he never does anything until he first dreams.   —William Rainey Bennett

———

Any Fool Can Destroy. It Takes an Architect, Brains, Ability, Materials to Build.

———

All Big Men Translate Sentimental Dreams into Realities.

———

Any Fool Can Throw up a Shack, but It Takes an Architect to Build a Ten-Story Skyscraper.

———

Reason, Like Steel, Is Kept Bright by Use or It Will Rust.

———

When You Get a large Grasp of Things, You Find the World Is Big Enough to Hold Those who Disagree.

All Depends upon What you Think when You See. All See Same Objects.

———

Some Minds Seem to Create Themselves, Springing up under Every Disadvantage, Working their Solitary but Irresistible Way thru a Thousand Obstacles.

———

If we torture ourselves by stubborn mistakes and ignorant tragedy sufficiently, so we rouse ourselves to demand new creations, then Innate within will evolve.

———

Become optimistically dissatisfied, and then recreate—that is the map of Innate's journey.

———

Only those who see invisible Innate can do the educationally impossible.

———

Outer expression is a crude visible symbol of what is happening inside with Innate. What is Innate inside is divinely projected history.

———

6. Wisdom

A search for the term "wisdom," in the 18 chiropractic texts written between the years 1920-1952, reveals 265 mentions of the word.[1] Close to half of those instances come from one book, *Up From Below the Bottom*. In that book, Palmer expands on his theory of wisdom as a type of essence. He describes it on a developmental spectrum from education to knowledge to wisdom. To understand Palmer's definition of wisdom, his metaphor of an apple is a good place to start,

> Education is theory that apple is there, and knowledge is fact. To utilize apple for purpose for which intended, as food, we see, smell, taste, eat, digest, and it becomes part of us, which is to possess WISDOM of the apple.[2]

This wisdom comes from the Innate Intelligence as it is the substance and essence of all life and as noted earlier, the soul of the universe. To continue the metaphor, wisdom is the ripening of knowledge through action, through use. Palmer wrote,

> Knowledge comes from a superior—and man has no superior in education, but he has a superior in knowledge—his Innate Intelligence; and Innate Intelligence has a superior in knowledge in Universal Intelligence. Wisdom is knowledge gained; ripe wisdom is knowledge ripened into practicability of practical use.[3]

The ripening itself is the essence, the wisdom. He wrote,

> Wisdom is knowledge gone ripe. Ripeness is fulfillment of an intent or desire. Function of apple tree is to build an apple, and ripen it. When building a green apple, that is knowledge; when it ripens it is wisdom.[4]

And yet, in all of this, we should keep Palmer's context in the foreground; how Innate informs Educated *and* is expressed through the body, especially in the absence of subluxation. And therein lay his vision for the future,

> In next four, five, six, or seven hundred years, the principle for which we stand will spread. Mankind, generation after generation, will receive adjustments, will lose a vast amount of fictitious Education; superstitions and myths will be exploded; knowledge and wisdom will flow to surface. *It must come from inside, and that cannot occur until subluxations are adjusted.* It would not be proper to turn loose on the world a man with a subluxation. He must go thru process of adjustment and new growth.[5]

Knowledge is knowing a fact.

Wisdom is knowing what to do with that fact.

———

The Man Who Thinks Lives in a Little World of His Own.

———

Fools Find Fault; Wise Men Discover Virtues.

———

Humanity Cries for Light when They Do not Make Use of Light They Have.

———

It is while we are green we grow, and when we think we are ripe we begin to rotten.

— (Signed) Fellow Maggot.

———

Gushers are shallow. Be a deep well.

———

Mental indigestion is the result of too much raw logic.

———

A plum becomes a prune by evaporation.

We wish human beings became as valuable when they became prunes.

———

The pleasure of doing good is the only one that does not wear out.

———

You cannot expect to be both grand and comfortable.

———

If you have been wise and prudent, we congratulate you; unless you are unable to forget how wise and good you are, then we pity you.

Honesty is the ONLY policy.

————

Why pray cream on Sunday and live skimmed milk the rest of the week?

————

The mintage of wisdom is to know that rest is rust, and that real life is in love, laughter, and work.

————

Unassuming simplicity is an emblem of nobility.

————

An egotist is an "I" specialist.

————

To educate the child, begin with the grandparents.

————

You can't teach a young dog old tricks.

————

Most people, like trees, begin to die at the top.

————

All things worth while cannot be proven, and nothing that can be proven is worth while.

————

We are like children who repeat by rote the sentences of grandames and tutors, and as we grow older, of the men of talent and character they chance to see.

————

A wise man discovers where he was wrong; a fool proves himself right.

Profiting by experience is using the knowledge you have gained through failures.

———

A fire department is just as busy when answering a false alarm as it is when going to a real one.

———

General principles are generally wrong.

———

We thought if we could once get into a great place we would be great. We would have been—a great joke!

———

If Moses had retired, at the "ripe age" of seventy-nine, to a checkerboard in a grocery store, or to pitching horseshoes up the alley and talking about the "winter of sixty-eight," he would have been the seventeenth mummy on the thirty-fifth row in the green pickle-jar.

———

Everybody is doing one of three things: Holding his place, rattling down, or shaking up.

———

Our funeral is held right after we "finish."

———

"Getting to the top" is the world's pet peeve. There is no top. Every top we reach is the bottom of the next step up.

———

The man who bulges his muscles and puffs his chest in declaring he is the best man ever, is generally jazzing, kidding himself and whistling past his graveyard.

"Remarkable" things happen in foreign lands. One cannot see the "miracle" in his own town or time; or, seeing it, thinks it a commonplace because it happens to him. "No man is a hero to his valet."

———

We forget what we ought to remember and remember what we ought to forget.

———

The human mind should be an organized file rather than a disorganized pile.

———

Some miners will find, and then throw back into the stream, the precious ore of gold for which they have gone through hell, without ever knowing its presence or its nearness.

———

We know what we experience. We believe what others have gone thru.

———

Everything has an individuality, but individual differences lie in methods rather than principles.

———

The wise man produces more than he consumes; the foolish man consumes more than he produces.

———

We spend the first part of our lives ignoring the advice given us and the second half giving advice that others ignore.

———

A wise man never blows his knows.

Twelve things to remember:
The value of time
The success in perseverance
The pleasure of working
The dignity of simplicity
The worth of character
The power of kindness
The influence of example
The obligation of duty
The wisdom of economy
The virtue of patience
The importance of talent
The joy of originating

———

Everything comes and goes in cycles which are graded in kind and proceed in accordance with immutable law.

———

We are omnibuses in which our ancestors ride.

—Dr. Wm. S. Sadler,

Surgeon, Author, Lecturer, and Diagnostician

———

Humility Kneels in Dust, but Gazes to Skies.

———

He Who Brings Ridicule to Bear against Truth Find a Blade Without a Hilt.

—Landor

———

Deep Rivers Move with Majesty; Shallow Brooks Are Noisy.

There are many men today whose single purpose is to lead a double life.

———

Your Senses of Seeing, Hearing, Smelling, Tasting, and Feeling Are Evaluated by MIND. Use It!

———

A "Broadminded" Person Accumulates a Conglomeration of "Facts," Making It Impossible to Pass an Opinion upon Any Subject.

———

Where Men Alternate Work, Play, and Study in Right Proportions, Organs of Mind Are Last to Fail. Death for Such Has no Terrors.

———

It Is Better to Be More than Tolerant, Especially when a Wiser and Better Man Thinks Differently.   —Landor

———

It Is Common for Man to Hate what He Does not Comprehend.

———

No one can build less fire and logically expect more heat.

———

Serenity of Mind Can only Be Obtained by a Clear Conscience.

———

A handicap is no longer a liability when ability gives it the LIE-ability.

———

The fellow who lies out of a mistake has discovered perpetual motion.

———

A blank cartridge is as good as a loaded one until you shoot it off.
   —William Rainey Bennett, Lecturer, Philosopher, and Humorist

When the Preacher Goes Hunting for Fame the Wolf Needs no Invitation to the Fold.

———

Next to Knowing When to Seize Opportunity the Important Thing Is to Know when to Forego an Advantage.   —Beaconsfield

———

As Well Expect to Grow Stronger by always Eating, as Wiser by Reading. It Is Thought and Digestion that Make Books Serviceable and Give Health and Vigor to the Mind.   —Fuller

———

The Idea that Education Contacts Innate Is Wrong. Innate Contacts Education. This Idea that Education Contacts Universal Intelligence Is Wrong. Universal Intelligence Contacts Innate and Innate Contacts Education. This Idea that Education Must Tell Innate how to Run a Human Body Is Wrong. This Idea that Education Must Tell Universal Intelligence How to Run the World Is Wrong. Universal Intelligence Directed Functions of the World before You and We Were Educationally Born. It Will Do so after You and We Are Educationally Dead. Innate Intelligence Directs Functions of Composite Organized Natural Beings, Insane, Imbeciles, Morons, More than You and We Imagine. Get Wisdom! It Is later than You Think.

———

AN EGOTIST IS AN "I" SPECIALIST.

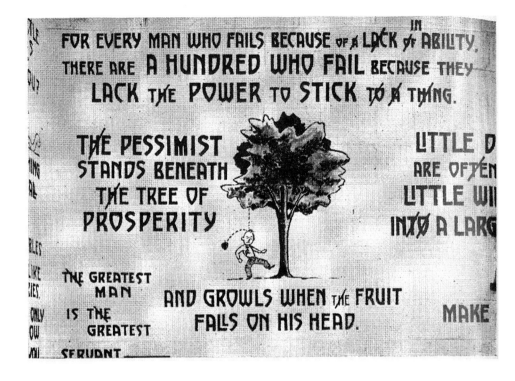

7. Food and Women

Palmer's writings on food and women are funny. This reproduction of Palmer's writings on women makes no attempt to be politically correct. It is my sincerest hope that no reader is offended. These epigrams are a reflection of the 1920s and 1930s. Some of them are quite entertaining...

Most of the epigrams about food were located in the Palmer School of Chiropractic cafeteria. The cafeteria was frequented by students and residents of Davenport. Palmer sometimes ate in the cafeteria with students. At the center of the cafeteria was water directly from the well, which was dug long before as the location of the building was once a farm. The best introduction to the writings on food is from Palmer's description of the cafeteria's business. Palmer wrote,

THE PSC owns and operates its own cafeteria.

It was opened April 16, 1920. In the year which followed we served:

10,950 gallons of soup.
200,750 pounds of meat, or over 100 tons.
3,285 bushels of potatoes.
9,125 gallons of brown sauce.
31,025 gallons of milk.
3,500 gallons of 30% cream.
21,900 pounds of butter.
13,688 gallons of salad.
54,570 loaves of bread.
7,800 pounds of coffee; or 23,400 gallons.

16,200 dozens eggs; or 54 dozen daily, or 194,400.
503,872 meals.
30-1/2 cents average cost, per meal.
131,313 customers at cigar and candy stand.
12-7/10 cents average sale.
37,256 customers at soda fountain.
16-7/8 cents average sale.
612,441 total of customers.[1]

By the old well—which is the one oddest thing to be found in any cafeteria in America—are found several carved slabs. On one is found. WELL! On another is found 'TIS WELL! On still another is found THIS IS WELL WATER!

———

It is better for us to eat together than each other.

———

The better the day,
The better the feed.

———

To eat is human,
To digest—divine!

———

If at first you don't fill up,
Try, try again!

———

My company 'tis of thee,
Hungry in-ter-nally,
Of thee I sing!

———

Onions make you strong physically, and weak socially.

———

Sleep where you please, but eat here.

———

Is wifey a bum cook? Eat here and keep her for a pet.

Eat, drink and be merry—for tomorrow you may diet!

———

Eat, drink and be merry, for each makes life worthwhile.

———

Because man was created first is no reason why woman should be considered a recreation.

———

When a man is chasing the almighty dollar, he forgets there is a God, and when he is chasing women he forgets there is a devil.

———

A married man is a male being, designed to do a female's bidding.

———

Just because Innate stopped work on some guys when Thon reached the Adam's apple, is no reason why we have to boast about it.

———

Sprinkling perfume on a skunk-cabbage won't make it a rose.

———

Some of the girls may be shallow thinkers, but they give us a cosmetic urge.

———

It seems that the best way to get your wife to take your advice is to have her elected a state governor.

———

Complaint is made that you can't tell one girl from another. But a good many fellows don't seem to want to.

———

Why is it that when a fellow isn't fresh they call him a good egg?

Too many young married people today think that a triangle is a good substitute for a fifty-foot front.

———

Did any man ever walk up the aisle of a girls, school without getting the feeling that his necktie had crawled 'way up behind?

———

It is true that all men are born free and equal but most of them get married.

———

When a woman tells the truth about her age she has given up hope.

———

It's better to have loved a short man than never to have loved a tall.

———

Eve was Adam's first "ribstake" but it cost him his grub-stake.

———

Anatomy Is Something Everyone Has but It Looks Better on a Girl.

———

The Tower of Babel Was where Solomon Kept his Wives.

———

Out West, Men and Women Wear Blue Jeans but OVER-ALL Effect Is Different.

———

On oak slab, over hat-rack: Better foods are impossible. Ur stomach can hold only 5 to 8 pints. With your cooperation we will reduce the cost. KEEP THE LOWER LINE A-MOVING.

She was only a build in a girdled cage!

———

We always feel like shooting the after-dinner speaker who reads a speech. If he can't remember it, how can he expect others to?

———

Woman was made from a rib and she's still a ticklish problem.

———

There's a woman on every dollar.
She makes love only to him who winks with system and smiles with service.

———

It's only the fresh egg that gets slapped in the pan.

———

Girdle—a Device to Keep a Woman Smaller on the Outside than She Is on the Inside.

———

Adam's First Day on Earth Was the Longest Because There Was no Eve.

———

Woman's fondness for dry goods and man's fondness for wet goods has wrecked many a home.

———

Is life worth living? That depends upon the liver!

———

ANATOMY IS SOMETHING
EVERYONE HAS
BUT IT LOOKS BETTER
ON A GIRL.

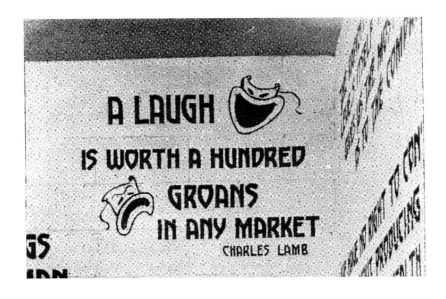

A LAUGH
IS WORTH A HUNDRED
GROANS
IN ANY MARKET
CHARLES LAMB

8. Self-Reliance

B.J. Palmer was a paragon of self-reliance. As with many great leaders, much of his development came through direct experience. Life was his greatest teacher and he knew it. His disdain for formal education is fascinating because he was president of Palmer College and the leader of a profession for almost 60 years. Palmer often opposed new state and professional regulations especially in regards to increasing educational standards. He initially viewed chiropractic as a trade, which all could learn. In order to meet the modern standards of professionalism and doctoral education, many others in the profession developed national standards, accrediting agencies, and boards. Palmer was forced to go along with the trends. Palmer wrote,

> We educate man ostensibly to make him useful. We cram him full of education to make him apparently useful. Paradox is true. More we educate, more useless he becomes. Hot-housing the human artificially forces that which should come naturally slower. More he educates *himself*, more useful he is. A man does not need go to school to educate himself, it is everywhere surrounding him if he will get it. Environment is full of facts. Big men at tops of ladders are self taught. Going to school doesn't hurt, but usually it makes the average man bad. Responsibility is gained by self-reliance. Responsibility is gained by individually assuming the thing.[1]

It is through self-reliance, especially when one could tap those infinite resources within, that true knowledge and wisdom are derived. Palmer wrote,

> No matter how many years we exist by cluttering up this earth on which we move and have our being, we will never reach maturity until such time as the educated fellow on the outside is as big and as great as the Innate inside.[2]

The criticism of the world is bitter only to those who cannot compel room for their ideas.

————

If you have no belief in yourself, how can you expect other people—your company, or your customer—to believe in you?

————

If you won't give yourself a square deal in little things, how can you expect one from the other fellow?

————

As we become better men, we become—just as surely—bigger men! It is man power that counts.

————

Other people's faith in you will be guided by your own faith in yourself, only.

————

No obstacle is big enough to stop the man who believes absolutely in himself and in his proposition.

————

A determined soul can do more with a rusty monkey-wrench than a loafer with a machine shop.

————

Many an orphan can be grateful that he was jolted from his life preserver and cruelly forced to sink or swim.

————

We are ashamed to think how easily we capitulate to badges and names, to large societies and dead institutions.

When you get the idea that the world is against you—it is.

———

For non-conformity the world whips you with its displeasure. And whosoever would be a man must know how to estimate a sour face.

———

The objection to conforming to usages that have become dead to you is that it scatters your force; it loses your time and blurs the impression of your character. Under these screens we have difficulty to detect the precise man you are.

———

My Religion:

I worship at the shrine of Freedom and Justice; kneel at the altar of Righteousness and Honor; humbly and reverently bow my head before Charity, Integrity and Truth. I never deny to another that which I demand for myself: the right to *think, act, worship or not worship,* according to the dictates of my conscience.

—Charles Reilly

———

Our religion is like others, man-made. But we are the man who made it.

———

We know you, if you have come up from the bottom.

———

Many men owe the grandeur of their lives to their tremendous difficulties.

———

Whoso would be a man, must be a nonconformist.

The growth and development you see here is the result of taking ourselves seriously while others took us as a joke.

―――

Man is timid and apologetic; he is no longer upright; he dares not say "I know," "I am," but quotes some saint or sage.

―――

Anything that you do that the majority do not do is "queer." Queer, isn't it?

―――

That man only is free who can divorce himself from "the recognized thing."

―――

We are as helpless as children, in a world of real things.

―――

Most men who are laboriously saving a few dollars would do better to invest them in themselves, and then in some useful work.

―――

In language, as in character and manners, simplicity is excellence supreme. Be yourself!

―――

If you are honest with yourself you need not utter special words in prayer.

―――

Most people are lost in a maze of illusions. They need to find themselves, with a vision.

―――

Blessed is that man who does not belliake.

It takes a soft people to put up with the necessity for soft coal.

———

There are nine leaners to one who can stand up.

———

We are daily becoming more conscious of the wonderful powers within us.

———

Romance of character and romance of experience come to those who let them alone. Self-consciousness dissipates romantic mystery.

———

No man can be serene who doubts himself.

———

As I read history, I do not find any people who have ever gone down through pressure from without.

—Arthur E. Bestor,
A.B., LL.D., Author, Educator, & President, Chautauqua Institute

———

"Think as We Do or You Are Wrong," Is Teaching of Fossils.

———

The Introvert Lives within a Small Narrow Circumscribed Vicious Circle of Educated Inbreeding, Boomeranging. The Extrovert Steps out of Educated Character, Absorbs the Great Unlimited Innate, Pushes Back Educated Horizon, and Becomes a new Personality.

Between These Is the Introvert with a Fake Extrovert Front. Beware. HE Is Dangerous.

Self-Reliance, Self-Respect, and Self-Control Are Three Things that Make a Man a Man.

———

There Are Exceptions to All Rules. Some People Delight in Being Exception Specialists.

———

A Boy Becomes an Adult Three Years before His Parents Think He Does—and about Two Years After HE thinks He Does.

———

Pleasure of Remodelling a Man Is in Reconstructing a Life.

———

Men with Well-Rounded Character Always Do Things on the Square.

———

The Work of Man-Building Is the Work of Life-Building.

———

Envy Is Meanest Form of Admiration. Man Who Envies Another Admits His Inferiority.

—Theodore Roosevelt

———

Be Fearful of Thyself and Stand in Awe of None More than Thine Own Conscience. There Is a Cato in Every Man, a Censor of His Manners, and He that Reverences This Judge Will Seldom Do Anything He Need Repent of.

———

Should We Have Gotten into Notice if We Had Waited to Be Hunted and Pushed by Older Men?

Tolstoi Says: "My Excuse for Thinking with my Own Head Is that I Have the Head of No One Else with which to Think."

———

Educated man is only animal that blushes—or needs to.

———

Measure of a man's character is what it should be if he knew he would never be found out.   —Maccauley

———

In Final Test It Makes Little Difference whether or not Others Believe in Us, but It Makes all the Difference in the World whether or not We Believe in Ourselves.

———

9. Affirmative

Palmer's focus on positive thinking was central to his attitude of success. Palmer claimed in 1950, that the phrase, "Keep Smiling," was a chiropractic slogan. He did not trust a man with a forced grin, but, he wrote, "I'll trust a man who can and does smile, because a smile is the reflection of the soul and the expression of an honest heart."[1] From the introduction to *As a Man Thinketh*,

> Dr. Palmer is a dominant and positive individual. He proves this by the nature of the affirmative epigrams everywhere. He believes in being constructive and everywhere is the builders, language. The only negatives are those which are so peculiarly worded that they are positive. "B. J." has realized, as has every other man who teaches the world its personal A, B, C's, that reading a thing repeatedly focuses its thot on the human mind. See it and you read it; read it and you think it; think it and it becomes you; becoming you, you are it—thus we build better, bigger, broader men and women."[2]

This positive attitude began before Palmer became a chiropractor. When he was about 17 years old, Palmer went on tour with a stage-hypnotist Herbert Flint and his daughter Marina.[3] From them, Palmer learned showmanship, confidence, the art of self-hypnosis, deep concentration, positive thinking, and how to access deep reservoirs of the self. Palmer wrote,

Week after week his positive suggestions gradually seeped in. We TRIED to accept, receive, and act upon them. AND THAT WAS THE TURNING POINT OF OUR CAREER—THAT WE TRIED! Eventually, Herbert and Marina taught us the EXTREME value of giving and receiving positive suggestions; how to receive and how to act. When we LEARNED THAT LESSON, WE TOOK THE DERELICT AND REBUILT HIM INTO SOMETHING WORTH WHILE.

From then on, we insistently and consistently trained our mind to follow that line of thinking. THAT laid a solid foundation upon which rest of our life has been moulded. Gradually, we rebuilt a, positive attitude towards life, thinking and acting. Gradually, we took the weak, insipid being we were and re-formed him into a strong dominant character. THE ROYAL ROAD TO HELL was wrong. THE ROYAL ROAD TO HEALTH was true. We could do anything we wanted to do if we wanted to long enough and strong enough. "WE WILL" became a line of reasoning:...[4]

Keep Smiling!

———

Harmony, Happiness and Health

———

Adjustment is the issue.

———

A smile on the face of some people reminds us of the top layer of apples in a box.

———

Love, laugh and live longer.

———

Let him who wins it bear the palm.

———

Believing in the power and effect of affirmation, we say the things we want to do. Having committed ourselves to a definite course, then it's up to us to live up to it.

———

2 B Constructive, B Affirmative, 2 B Destructive, B Negative.

———

Still water doesn't run deep. It's standing still.

———

{A-bility } Personality {R-eliability } {E-ndurance } = {H-ead, Heart, Hand}

———

We would like to be responsible for your hats and coats, but how can we?

Distinctividuality

———

Cooperation is the thing.

———

An optimist is one who sees a light where there is none. A pessimist is one who blows it out.

———

Smile and smile often, smile regularly, smile when you don't feel like it and you will feel like it when you smile.

———

The Glory of Going On.

———

An optimist is one who makes sandwiches, while it rains, for a picnic to which they won't go. A pessimist is one who eats them at home.

———

It's better to be optimistically dissatisfied than pessimistically satisfied.

———

A pessimist is one who has the choice of two evils and chooses both.

———

Troubles Are like Babies—They only Grow if You Nurse Them.

———

There's no Time Like the Pleasant.

———

Cheerfulness Is Normal Condition of Well Men with Open Minds, Warm Hearts, Square Shoulders, and no Fear of the Dark.

Enthusiasm Is the Genius of Sincerity. Truth Accomplishes Victories.

—Bulwer

———

This old world we're livin' in Is mighty hard to beat. We get a thorn with every rose, But ain't the roses sweet!

———

Life is the Great Adventure. Each day brings some new, interesting experience.

———

The One Who Looks up Sticks.

———

Wrinkles Ought to Be Places Where Smiles Belong.

———

Defeat Isn't Bitter unless You Swallow It.

Man, Like a Watch, Is Valued by Manner of His Going.

—Penn

———

A Laugh Is Worth a Hundred Groans in any Market.

—Charles Lamb

———

By Entertaining Good Thoughts You Keep Out Evil Ones.

———

Thru Meekness Overcome Anger; thru Goodness, Bad; thru Generosity, Miser; thru Truth, Liar.

———

The World Likes a Hopeful, Sunny, Buoyant Character, Shunning Gloomy Prophets who See Failure and Disaster Ahead.

The Greatest Thing in the World Is Where We Stand and in what Direction We Are Going.

———

Every Great and Commanding Movement Is the Triumph of Enthusiasm.   —Emerson

———

Tell People You Are a Failure and They Believe You. Talk and Act Like a Winner. In Time You Will Become One.

—Stephen Harte

———

When you start being grateful for something you have taken for granted, that's one step towards better side of your ledger.

———

Better to Light one Candle than to Curse Darkness.

10. Advertising

Advertising was one of Palmer's great strengths. From his first full-page ad in 1903, where he proclaimed he had the "CURE," which almost landed him in jail, to his books and lectures on advertising, Palmer's advertising acumen was essential to chiropractic's early success. Advertising was one of the keys. Palmer wrote,

Advertise? If your business isn't worth being advertised, then advertise it for sale. The New Success Magazine recently was authority for this: "Of all the failures recorded in 1920, 84% were of firms that did not advertise." Isn't it funny? Man wakes up in the morning, after sleeping under an advertised blanket, on an advertised (Ostermoor) mattress; takes off advertised pajamas; takes a shower in an advertised (Crane Co.) tub; shaves with an advertised (Gillette) razor; washes with advertised (Ivory) soap; powders his face with an advertised (Mennen's) powder; dons advertised underwear, (Hole-proof) hose, shirt (E. & W.), collar, (Douglas) shoes, (Hart Shaffner & Marx) suit, (Sealkerchief) handkerchief; sits down to breakfast of an advertised (Postum) cereal; drinks advertised (Yuba) coffee; puts on an advertised (Stetson) hat; lights an advertised (Owl) cigar; rides to his office in an advertised (Ford) car on advertised (Goodrich) tires, where he refuses to advertise on the grounds that advertising does not pay. "It is only the fool, any more, who denies the influence of advertising."[1]

In the introduction to his 1926 version of the short book, *Selling Yourself*, Palmer describes why he is eminently qualified to teach on the subject of selling yourself. He begins with the stories of his difficult early years and continues by describing his nightly radio talks about his world travels, listened to by millions. He wrote,

All of this is mentioned here that you might know that whatever is said comes from the University of Hard Knocks, chiseled bit by bit, year after year. It's the hard-boiled truth handed to you in no equivocal language. It's told you in pungent, terse, perhaps uncalled for words, but what is said comes from one who speaks with knowledge. This is no bookworm who speaks, one who reads and then mockingly repeats, but one who has wrested success from Mother Nature and Father Time; who has climbed the ladder from below the bottom to somewhere up near the top. It is not a didactic exposition second-handed, nor does the college profession hand you much—here you get facts without mercy; language without looseness; truths that hurt.[2]

He that bloweth not his own horn, for him shall no horn be blown.

———

Only the mints can make money without advertising.

———

When anybody about here ceases to call us "B.J." then we need to sell ourself again and again.

———

The hen cackles all day just to be properly heard when the farmer comes out once.

———

"Early to bed, early to rise,"
Work like hell—and advertise,
"Makes a man healthy, wealthy and wise."

———

Yes. I believe in signs!

———

What you want to keep out of a newspaper is news. What you want to get into a newspaper is an advertisement.

———

Build a better mouse trap than your neighbor, use printers' ink and tell the world, and even tho you live in the midst of a wilderness, the world will then beat a path to your door to get it.

———

The man who whispers to the few
About the things that he can do,
Will never "cop" the big round dollars
Like he who scatters cards and hollers.

"Mary had a little lamb." But we'd never know it if she had not advertised.

————

Where ignorance is happiness, it is unbecoming to be wise.

————

Pessimism is negative, denial, believing that evil is more than good, that life is not worth death; it is a dampening down. Pessimism tends to annihilation because it takes away life's motives, vigor and power. *Optimism* is positive, it cheers, brightens, encourages, beautifies, glorifies, blesses, helps. We have learned that that man who succeeds, helps, benefits and blesses mankind, is essentially an optimist.

————

Better vanity, if you will, than sham modesty.

————

Invention is the mother of necessity.

————

Advertising is to business what the brass band is to the parade. It is also true that a parade can go through the streets without a brass band, but who would see it?

————

There's no fool like a sold fool.

————

Good advertising is a salesman talking to hundreds of customers at once.

————

Ads are the nervous system of the business world.

Nine People Will Believe Nine Lies before One Person Will Believe One Truth.

—Nugent

———

Those Who Sing Own Praise Need Expect no Encore.

—Ryland

———

If You Want Money for Things You Sell, Build REASONS why Customers Should Buy Them.

———

Hens cackled some time before somebody realized that eggs were good to eat.

———

BUSINESS IS A STATE OF MIND.
SUCCESSFUL BUSINESS IS AN ANALYSIS
OF THAT STATE OF MIND.
ONE LAW. MANY PRINCIPLES. MORE RULES.

11. Business

Palmer's business success is obvious. In the 1950s, he was listed as one of the builders of America. As an example of the reach of his life; in the famous Grove Park Inn in my hometown of Asheville, NC, his portrait hangs on the wall of photos with presidents and celebrities. Palmer's picture is currently framed with Will Rogers and Eleanor Roosevelt. It was in his business success that Palmer was able to thrive and forward his vision most completely. He took the lessons he learned from his early days with Professor Flint, the hypnotist, and applied it to business. Palmer wrote,

Successful business men use "self-hypnosis" on themselves.

Successful business men use hypnosis in positive suggestions to others....

Every SUCCESSFUL business man today knowingly or unknowingly uses hypnosis in presenting positive suggestions to buyer.... Ability to transplant YOUR thots into mind of buyer-customer by use of positive suggestions, and get him to act upon it by buying, is THE KEY to all sales success. WE use it every day. Every business man who climbs the ladder uses it. He must if he is to get ahead of mass of buyers.[1]

In his later years, he relied more and more on his ability to listen to Innate and use those thought-flashes to lead his business endeavors. It seems even the executives in his businesses learned to listen to B.J.'s Innate. Palmer wrote,

Many times, some of our educated people in our Palmer Enterprises tell US not to do this this way, but do it that way, meaning of course WE should follow THEIR educated methods of presentation. At such times, we must decide whether to follow suggestions offered by our Innate by preference, rejecting THEIR educated presentations. When they remain with us long enough, they will learn the LAW OF INNATE'S PRESENTATIONS. When they DO, they will understand why we feel it necessary to reject their educated opinions.[2]

Business is a state of mind. Successful business is an analysis of that state of mind.

———

Confidence is the backbone of business.

———

It was the business managers of the country and not the medical fraternity who discovered the symptoms of "sleeping sickness."

———

Never mind the business outlook. Be, on the outlook for business.

———

Take a firm interest in your firm's interest and the firm will take a firmer interest in you.

———

To the fellow who shows up late, and sneaks home early, we are indebted (?) for the "punch clock" system.

———

You are a part of the organization as much as the bass drum is a part of the orchestra—likewise, remember that bass drum solos are monotonous.

———

The psychologist who remarked that "the average American is dead from the neck up" ought to watch some of the girls chew gum.

———

Believing in people is just as essential as believing in our product, or, in ourselves.

———

A Wise Merchant Takes Stock of Himself as Well as His Goods.

———

To Be a Great Sales Manager, Be a Dynamo and Send out Electricity of Enthusiasm.

———

Many a Business Man Has Gone to Pieces on Rocks because He Was Lacking Sand.

———

There are just two reasons for not minding one's own business: First, because one has no business to mind; and second, because one has no mind.

———

Worship of Precedent Is Death of Business.

———

Business is inherently hostile to law, because business travels faster.

———

A thing that is bought or sold has no value unless it contains that which cannot be bought or sold. Look for the Priceless Ingredient. What is that? It is the Honor and Integrity of him who makes it.

———

Revenues increase arithmetically, but expenses increase geometrically.

———

When the man of business, be it in barrels or brains, hands his slogan in the marts he that moment becomes a person of purpose and a sponsor of standards. If he is not a fool he knows his reputation is at stake.

———

In industry, nothing is impossible. In industry, everything is possible.

Any idea, person or institution that is based upon a product, service or demand of the people, that is so new, original, peculiar or queer that it INTERRUPTS the reader, overcomes inertia, compels investigation and creates action.

———

It requires less skill to make a fortune dealing in money, than dealing in production.

———

Digging wells is the only business where you can begin at the top.

———

You may begin business in any obscure place, but if there is ability, power and mastery of affairs, then all the steamboats will whistle for you, and the railroads say, "Come over and manage us." You cannot be hidden. If you have nothing the world wants, no power to paint a picture or manage a business, you may live in your front window and drive on Fifth Avenue, but you are hidden.

———

To rest content with results achieved is the first sign of business decay.

———

Most anyone can run a job when things are going smooth. The demand is for the fellow who's equal to the occasion when things strike a snag.

———

The fellow who wants time off with pay is generally the first one to demand time and a half for overtime.

———

The telephone service never gets to such a pitch of inefficiency that the company can't reach you with a bill.

———

The student or customer always was right, always is right and always will be right!

———

To buy below actual value is not honesty!
To sell below cost is unfair competition!

———

Many a big business got started on a shoe string.

———

"Time, tide and WOC wait for no man."

———

The only man who ever built a business on "bunk" is Geo. Pullman.

———

9 A. M. to 5 P. M.—Union hours.
5 A. M. to 9 P. M.—Successes.

———

Make Man Normal and Business Will Take Care of Itself.

———

Man who Steals Employer's Time Is as much a Thief as the Man who Steals Money. Honest Man Will Give His Employer an Honest Day's Work.

———

Seest Thou a Man Diligent in Business? He Shall Stand before Kings; He Shall not Stand before Mean Men.   —Proverbs of Solomon

Ruin which Overtakes Many Merchants Is Due to Lack of Business Talent and to Lack of Business Nerve.

———

Laborer Who Works to Get Higher Is Laborer Who Is Worthy of His Hire.

———

It Is Harder to Be a Successful Hypocrite than a Sincere, Honest Worker in the World's Productive Shops, Factories, Printeries, or Offices. Accomplishment Is more Pleasurable than Deceitful "Soldiering."

———

Team work is important. Even a banana gets skinned when it leaves the bunch.

———

Time is money—many take this literally and undertake to pay debts with it.

———

Over the cashier's desk is found this paraphrase: THERE ARE BILLS THAT MAKE US HAPPY! which is a takeoff on the song, "There are smiles that make us happy, there are smiles that make us sad."

———

Anything that pays for itself is worth all it costs.

———

12. Excellence

Palmer valued hard work and striving to excel. Add to that the ability to tap into one's potential, and excellence emerges. This view is exemplified in the epigrams as well as his writings on genius. Palmer wrote,

…He studies the "prodigy," the "genius." Why do THEY excel along certain lines over the vast majority? Where do THEY get special talents? Is there something all can do to attain the same qualifications and duplicate such arts?

We know all men and women are created alike, a common pattern, therefore the mental patternmaker in all is alike. As the product, so the producer. In and behind our common race is a common intelligence which conceives, develops, gives birth and directs all functions alike once they become separate units. That common source is alike in all—that IS EVIDENCE we should educationally fathom. Then, where lies this discriminatory feature that sets ONE out prominently and subdues another into a background?

Ask these individuals "How do you do WHAT you do, AS you do it?" Answer is simple. "I don't know. It just comes." The same common internal source to all, thot-flashes ideas to one below who accepts them, acts upon them, yields to their intents and desires; the other seeks and does not understand. Each has same thot-flashes if he will listen to that wee-sma' voice in the same way. It might be music, painting, poetry, new inventions; in fact, such thot-flashes encompass everything every person has conceived and portrayed. He recognizes EVIDENCE of external contact in another, why not in himself? EVIDENCE of WHY and HOW one succeeds, the other fails, is that he has been "educated" to question, deny, debate, argue, challenge the subtle when they flash thru from within into his "education" in his outer stages of thinking.[1]

When love and skill work together, expect a masterpiece.

———

We'll grub-stake any man digging for truth and move all hell to dump error overboard.

———

Some people are so afraid they will go to hell when they die, that they make a hell on earth while they live.

———

All progress comes from the pursued, not the pursuer.

———

Egotism is the opiate that Innate administers to deaden the pains of mediocrity.

———

Half our life is spent in getting competents to repair the botchwork of incompetents.

———

The inefficients are the most costly members of society.

———

The world's progress is held back by just one thing—our universal unwillingness to grow.

———

Following the paths of least resistance is what makes rivers and men crooked.

———

Get out and hustle or be hustled out.

———

Constant striving to make our best, better.

It is easy to live after the world's opinion. It is easy in solitude to live after our own; but the great man is he who in the midst of the crowd keeps, with perfect sweetness, the independence of solitude.

———

A college education shows a man how little other people know and how much more he has to learn.

———

Another good thing about telling the truth is, you don't have to remember what you say.

———

We need to be reminded now and then that the world has rationalized beyond men to man, that we must measure performances and powers by the net result to our heads, hearts and hands, not alone by our pile of dollars and dimes.

———

Jesus was thirty years getting ready to do three years' work. So many prospective chiropractors expect to get ready in "four easy lessons by mail," "at home," "earn while you learn."

———

We believe that the man worth while cares more for results than for how much a day.

———

From this day on, we mean to do the best we can. If we are right, time will prove it. If we are not right, ten angels swearing we are right will not make it so.   —Abraham Lincoln

By the time you think you have made both ends meet, somebody moves the ends.

———

All experience accumulates; do the same amount, or more—but do it more easily.

———

People Seldom Improve when They Have no Model Other than Themselves to Copy.   —Goldsmith.

———

A Trained Man Will Make His Life Tell. Without Training You are Left on a Sea of Luck, where Thousands Go Down while One Meets with Success. Training, with Brain Work, Is what Brings Success.

—James A. Garfield

———

The world wants art, not a lark; skill, not swill; service, not swagger.

———

Any plan which starts with the assumption that men are or ought to be equal is unnatural, therefore unworkable.

———

Forcing the efficient producer to become inefficient does not make the efficient producer more efficient.

———

Destiny is the one artificer who can use all tools and find shortcuts to his goal through ways mysterious and most devious.

———

The Glory of tomorrow is rooted in the Drudgery of today.

Conventionality is an imitation of environment.

———

Way for a Young Man to Rise Is to Improve Himself, Never Suspecting Anybody Wishes to Hinder Him.

———

You enjoy singing; and, it isn't whether the singing is good or bad! That isn't what counts, at all. It's whether the singer puts anything that is hers (or his) into the thing. The best singers are those who put the most of themselves into what they try to sing.

We have heard people and crowds sing (and we use the word despairingly) who couldn't sing but it sounded like the voices of angels. Their souls, hearts, minds and all that was they were in it. We have heard other famous singers who warbled like trained parrots to repeat certain notes written by the ancients who no more sang than any Victrola we have heard. They sang (and we use the word despairingly) like records—made a noise.

Music isn't what it is, or how nice it is, or how perfect it is being repeated. Music is what the person puts into it.

When you sing, put all you've got into it; and, no matter how poor, it's music to you. It develops something otherwise latent; it drags out, it draws from within the things you feel and gives expression thereto.

So, when any other person is trying to bring out that which they actually feel, applaud the effort; for in the effort comes the development that makes for greater men and women. Applaud them!

So, whether you have a "voice" or not, whether you can "properly place the tone" in the right place in your nose or not; whether you have strong, vibrant tones or not, open up and let it all come out no matter how bad. Make a noise, whistle, hum, sneeze it if you please—give vent! It's the putting the mental-steam into it that makes you feel better. Applaud yourself for trying.

So, when a singer sings, or but tries, you have two hands that God gave you to make manifest your appreciation. The very fact that you pat your hands together, makes you see better than you heard. It puts tone to that which might not have had any. Anyhow, music is just what you think it is. Applaud and it will be more than it was!

———

The man who has won and will retain his place has come to where he is because he paid the price.

———

Every man in the world who is at the top of any ladder has paid all the gate fees.

———

Some men who are at the top of the ladder have been checked thru on passes but they will back out thru the rear exits before the show is over.

———

You advance in life according to the time you spend that you do not get paid for.   —Sherman Rogers, Associate Editor "Success" Magazine, President, Optimist International

———

Show me what every man does from seven o'clock until eleven o'clock in the evening, and I will show you where he is going to be.

—Sherman Rogers

The Time You Succeed Is the Last Time You Try.

―――――

Have Confidence; Impress Your Cranium You Can Do as Well as Your Competitor, and Prove It.   —Albright

―――――

Many a Man Thinks He Is Working Hard when He Wabbles Between Duty and Desire.

―――――

We Lose Great Attainment when We Turn It into a Resting Place.

―――――

Strive Against Your Inferior and You Proclaim Him Your Equal.

―――――

The Man who Halted on Third Base to Congratulate Himself Failed to Make a Home Run.

―――――

What Is Your Best? You Can Answer this By Trying Harder than You Tried Before.

―――――

Talent of Success Is Doing what You Can Well, without a Thought of Fame.   —Longfellow

―――――

To Give Information—Sell an Article—Carry Out a Plan— Know. To Get Results—Know Facts.

―――――

The World Admires Those who Do what Nobody Else Attempts, and Those Who Do Best what Multitudes Do Well.

Discontent Is a Never-Ceasing Current of Reproach that Refuses to Let Stream of Energy Pause and Stagnate. It Counteracts Inertia; Vanishes Smug Satisfaction; Jeers at "Little" Achievement.

———

If Men Are Nearly Equal, One Who Is Enthusiastic Tips Scales in His Favor.

———

Ceasing to Do New Things and Think New Thoughts—
That Is Growing Old.

———

Rest Satisfied with Doing Well, and Leave Others to Talk as They Please.   —Pythagoras

———

Do It Better! Letting Well Enough Alone Never Raised a Salary or Declared Extra Dividend. What Was Well Yesterday is Poor Enough Today — Do It Better. Strive to Surpass.

———

13. Koan

A Zen-koan is a statement or question designed to thrust the conscious mind into a profound realization of the nondual nature of reality, the oneness and manyness that is all things. Zen masters would tell a story, make a statement, or ask a question triggering a state of enlightenment in the student. A classic Koan is, "What is the sound of one hand clapping?" If the student attempts to respond from the rational thinking mind, the answer is incorrect. Only a response demonstrating the student's depth of insight into the paradoxical nature of reality, a deep form of spiritual awakening, is "right." Palmer's contemplation of the relationship between Innate, Universal and chiropractic was a lifelong koan, a contemplation of the deepest mysteries of creation and how the human relates to such or suchness. Palmer wrote,

> "God", no matter how defined, is omnipresent, omniscient, omnipotent, INSIDE of man in THE CREATION OF MAN. **Where** is this IN man at all? **If** it is, this all pervading INTERNAL power must be recognized and established as a dominant factor in healing WITH man, sick or well.[1]

These are the types of questions Palmer utilized to teach the depths of the truth he and his father developed. Another example,

All therapies admit that "nature cures," "nature heals." Where does "nature" come from? Where is it? Can it be found in a teaspoon or out of a bottle? Is it found by ripping out necessary organs? Is it a force artificially manufactured to be artificially injected? Is it foreign thinking, taught by one educated man to another? Is it something externally foreign to itself which must come from the outside in? Or, was it inside when the body was healthy and is still there when the body is sick, which can be restored from where it is inside to where it isn't inside? Is it something *natural* that must come from within?[2]

In the following epigrams, I only chose the ones that short circuited my brain. These are different than wisdom epigrams, which were wise. As I read each of the following quotes, I could not make sense of them with my rational mind, my *Educated*. I had to connect with my "soul's knowing" to have meaning emerge. If I tried to explain that meaning with my Educated, I could not convey the depth. Words cannot truly capture the transrational because words are inherently rational. They can only point to it as in poetry or koans or stories. The moon should not be mistaken for the finger pointing to it.

The art of remembering is the gentle art of forgetting.

———

We need not so much to realize the ideal as to idealize the real.

———

The relations of the soul to the divine spirit are so pure that it is profane to seek to interpose helps.

———

Man is a reasoning, very unreasonable manifestation of divine intelligence.

———

Man does not stand in awe of men, nor is the soul admonished to stay at home, to put itself in communication with the internal ocean, but it goes abroad to beg a cup of water of the urns of men.

———

Man is a great big soul carrying around a little stubborn matter.

———

Right now you are making a choice to become a disappearing fossil or join the great forward Innate parade.

———

Be not Alarmed as to Great Truth. It May Be Obscured for a Time by Error, but Always to Rise in Greater Glory.

———

Only the watchman or the watch repairer can watch the watch and make a go of it.

———

Man is still in the process. He has not yet arrived.

You all belong to our church; we could not exclude you if we would. But if we should shut you out, we would then close the doors upon ourself and be a prisoner, indeed.

———

What is Mind? Never Matter! What is Matter? Never Mind!

———

This word — IN-TEL-A-DAF-OR-UN-I-TY — confuses many people. In plain Yankee it means INTELlectual ADAptation of FORce UNits producing UNITY. It is a compound word formed from the first letters of many. In-tel-a-daf-or-un-i-ty.

———

Not—how little for how much,
But—how much for how little.

———

All things are dissolved to their center by their cause, and in the universal miracle petty and particular miracles disappear.

———

The just, scientific mind goes beyond its own conditions of time and space. It builds itself an observatory erected upon the border of present, which separates the infinite past from the infinite future.

———

Time Scratches Every Itch.

———

One law, many principles, more rules.

———

It is not enough to make both ends meet; they must overlap.

An egotist knows everything; an egoist knows that he knows nothing.

———

To know is to disbelieve. When we disbelieve, we know.

———

The double-standard of morals is a crime for the goose, but a pasture for the gander.

———

Who can anchor to an unanchored mind?

———

(Yesterday) . . . What'll ya have?
(Today) . . . . . . Where'd ya get it?

———

The wheel that needs grease, is the one which squeals.

———

It's a great game, if you don't waken.

—Rip Van Winkle

———

Compromise and subterfuge are ingredients inseparable from the illusions of the near.

———

Few Prophets Will Bet on the Result.

———

"Whatever Is, Is Right." Evidently the Author Never Knew What It Was to Get Left.

———

Can You Tell a Live Wire from a Dead One by Looking at It?

Wrap Mind about Thing You Do; Study, Analyze, Finger It with Tentacles of Your Brain. Concentrate so Long that All Parts and Details Stand before You.

———

> **MAN IS A REASONING VERY UNREASONABLE MANIFESTATION OF DIVINE INTELLIGENCE**

14. Funny

The funny epigrams speak for themselves. Instead of commenting on them or providing an apt quote, I would like to share one of my favorite of Palmer's stories. He wrote,

How the Law Works

On December 18, 1948, we had to go to Des Moines, 186 miles from Davenport. Should we drive or go by train? The 15th, 16th, and 17th of December were beautiful, sunshiny days, ideal for driving. On the 15th, Innate told me to go my train. Reservations were made accordingly.

At 8:00 A.M. on the 18th, it began to drizzle; it froze; the roads were sheets of ice. It snowed all day, on top of the ice. Roads were "extremely hazardous" and warnings were issued to "keep off all highways." Innate knew!

The train was packed—holiday travelers. Arriving in Des Moines, there were more than a hundred people waiting for taxis. There was only one, and it was loaded and off before we arrived at the taxi stand. It was cold, wind was blowing, and we thought we might have to wait an hour for a taxi, for on such occasions taxis are at a premium. For a moment my educated mind didn't know what to do. The next moment I said, "Innate will provide; she always does!"

One minute after reaching the taxi stand, a private car drove up. "Are you Dr. Palmer?" I replied I was. "Can I give you a lift somewhere?" We piled in. On our way to the hotel, this man said, "When I was six, I suffered terribly with earache. I tried all kinds of doctors and drugs. None did me any good.

Finally, I went to one of your graduates—Dr. Julander, in Des Moines. In a few days my earache was gone and now I am a married man and I've had no earache since. I take my family to this Chiropractor now whenever there is anything wrong. I am a 'C.B.' (Chiropractic Booster). I recognized you from your picture hanging in his office. It is a pleasure to return any favor to you."

Innate worked years ago from us through this Chiropractor, Dr. Julander. Innate has worked through this particular Chiropractor for thirty-five years, he never deviating from the Innate principle and practice; therefore, Innate worked in the patient, relieving his earache. This patient, having taken adjustments, was a better receiver; therefore, it worked on this occasion through him, for us.

As we drove past the Equitable Life Insurance Building, I said: "In that tower WHO has its FM transmitter." He replied, "That's the company in which I am an executive."

Many will say this was coincidence, accident, luck, just happened. To the majority, it would be that. When "incidents" like this "happen" consistently and persistently, time without end, year after year, under many varied conditions, it becomes a law at work.[1]

Signs few believe in—

Keep off the grass.

Let us feed the fish; we know how.

Admittance is by pass only.

He's busy now.

Private property.

No trespassing.

Pull the latch string.

Keep out—This means you.

Stop! They're broadcasting now.

Wet paint.

Silence.

No children admitted to recitals.

Painless dentist.

No applause, Please.

Artists must arrive before 6:45.

———

He who laughs longest, laughs last.

———

In the employees, toilet is found this one:
Deliver your message to Garcia.

———

Where there is will, there are relatives.

———

The sheriff put many a man on his feet by taking away his car.

———

They will talk anyway.

When worm turns, it may be because he got instructions from back seat.

———

A Man Is not a Good Musician when He Goes Out Fit as Fiddle and Returns Tight as a Drum.

———

People and pins are useless when they lose their heads.

———

Many people suffer with a constipation of thot and a diarrhea of words.

———

They say! What say they? Let them say.

———

The lobster is the only animal who travels backward to go forward. He belongs to the old school.

———

Remember the week (weak) day to keep it holy.

———

Beauty is only skin deep—and many people need peeling.

———

"Bitter taste in the mouth." Where else could it be? (Goat-feather.)

———

If at first you don't suck seed, keep sucking till you do.

———

When the bored say the wrong thing to the right person at the wrong time, then things will liven up a bit.

An Irishman fights before he reasons; the Scotchman reasons before he fights; but the American Union isn't particular as to the order, but will do either to accommodate the calamity agitator.

———

The inscription on the wall of the room from which the chimes are played, uses musical language:

Sometimes be sharp—never be flat—always be natural.

———

A four-sided, square-toed man is so rare that when the wobbly world sees one thru its eyes, he's too good to be true.

———

The poorest sort of monopoly for any man to undertake is goat feathers.

———

Where there is a will, there are 40 ways.

———

If you are a mouthy Mexican matador, acute or chronic, mount, tie your long-horned Durham outside, then enter.

———

There are ten literary drunkards to one alcoholic drunkard. There are one hundred bookworm drunkards to one booze slave.

———

All things come to those who wait—but there're too durn many waiting.

———

Most people die early, tickled to death reading their own press notices.

The come-hither-in-your-eye.

———

Man is highly specialized and organized mud, and is occasionally being run by a highly specialized and organized mind.

———

Allegro, non too mucho.

———

We may be foolish enuf to be a fool, but we are having a lot of fun playing the game.

———

Nobody invites you? Perhaps you swipe electric globes, hotel towels and strike matches on our walls.

———

A crease in the kabeza is worth nine in the pants.

———

If ten bachelors of art were shipwrecked in mid-ocean they could not build a pontoon to save their lives.

———

You can throw bouquets at yourself, but they do not have the authentic fragrance.   —Dr. Joseph Jastrow,

Prof. of Psychology, University of Wisconsin

———

The highbrows are now discussing the function of the critic. Generally it is to muddy up the hole when the big game are away.

———

It is almost as much trouble trying to think up excuses for missing engagements as it is to keep the engagements.

Blessed is the frog that stays under water. He saves his head and hide from being hit.

———

One nice thing about going to heaven will be not having any neighbors with an automatic piano living about you. And in hell no one underneath can kick to the landlord if you want to dance a little.

———

Scientists can prove that we are descended from monkeys and prove it to everybody's satisfaction—but monkeys.

———

Some people sit and think but many just sit.

———

The inventor of the mirror was fortunate. He could look ahead and see nothing in it.

———

Yes—Myrt—some folks hate bathin' suits because they sacrifice modesty. But we love 'em for the way they ruin dignity.

———

If You Had to Live Your Life Over, Chances Are You Would Make a Different Kind of Fool of Yourself.

———

Because Darwin Claims We Descended from Monkeys Is no Reason for Making Monkeys of Ourselves.

———

Some Men Would Look more Spic if They Didn't Have so much Span.

———

Helofafix.

Obesity Is Surplus Gone to Waist.

———

People desiring to be served in the cafeteria line up alongside of the windows. On the inside of the window casing, facing them as they pass down, are these words: Kuli-Kuli Wiki-Wiki, which, in the language of the Hawaiian, means: Kuli-Kuli—Shut-up! Wiki-Wiki—Hurry up!

———

Dieting Is the Art of Letting Hips fall Where they May. It is Triumph of Mind over Platter. Will Power Usually Is Greater than Won't Power.

———

Man Has 66 Pounds of Muscle and 3 Pounds of Brains. That Explains Lots of Things.

———

A bird in the hand is bad table manners.   —Cornell Widow

———

When it comes to buying perfume, you pay through the nose.

———

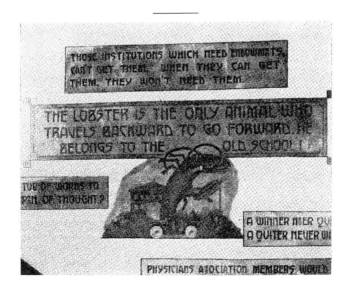

15. Chiropractic

As the son of the first chiropractor and president of the first chiropractic school from 1906 to 1961, B.J. Palmer *was* chiropractic. His own definitions of chiropractic evolved as he did. In the earliest years, it was defined according to his father's ideas. As the profession was challenged in the courts, B.J. was forced to develop definitions that ensured chiropractic's uniqueness as a profession. Yet, at the core of chiropractic was the philosophy and understanding that when conditions were right, the body heals itself within the limitations of the physical matter. Palmer wrote, "While other professions are concerned with changing environment to suit the weakened body, Chiropractic is concerned with strengthening the body to 'suit' environment."[1]

As the years went on and Palmer's research and practice continued, the definition of chiropractic evolved. The chiropractic adjustment, which was designed to release pressure from spinal nerves and the spinal cord allowed the innate intelligence to be expressed more fully. Vertebral subluxations resulted in a lack of expression of innate and this was deemed the cause of all dis-ease. As his ideas evolved, the adjustment and his understanding of it changed. In his later years, he sought to do as little as possible so the Innate Intelligence could do what it needed to. His definitions became more energetic because of his research. Palmer wrote,

"In the EVOLUTION of **all** adjusting, desire always has been to see how little invasionary force WE could use. —to see how much it made possible an Innate responsive reaction to set and seat the subluxation naturally and normally."[2]

Discovery Is Not Proof. A principle-constant was conceived by DD Palmer, in 1895, on a quantity flowing energy proposition. Would that conception prove true or untrue? - life is motion- there is no motion without energy to move matter - health is a rate of activity - if rate of speed of motion is normal – health - if slowed down – sickness and dis-ease - to reduce quantity flow of energy is to produce dis-ease - vertebral subluxation shorts energy flow - vertebral adjustment restores it and restores health.[3]

His definition expanded with his evolving conception of Innate and the energetic nature of the human organism. In his final book, Palmer wrote,

a. Chiropractic is a philosophy.
b. of the source and development of internal human function
c. from above-down, inside-out
d. the science of determining the location of
e. the interference to the flow of between source in brain and function in body
f. to the normal flow of mental impulses
g. thru the nervous system
h. and the art of adjusting vertebral subluxations.
i. by hand only
j. which produce pressures upon spinal cord or spinal nerves
k. to allow for restoration of a mental impulse flow
l. so that Innate Intelligence
m. resident within each living body
n. has a free full flow
o. in the re-establishment and restoration of health.[4]

Chiropractic is like a Xmas tree—if you don't put something ON, there won't be anything to take off.

———

Spizzerinctum!

———

A Chiropractoid has four speeds reverse and one speed ahead; he is a backslider! A Chiropractor has four speeds ahead and one speed reverse; he gives you a back-set!

———

Sleep will recruit rest; exercise will reduce laziness; adjustments will restore health. This prescription is good, but the masses do not heed it! They prefer to pay for a Latin order. Barnum was right!

———

Nothing that can be poured out of a bottle and taken with a spoon will take the place of a sawbuck—or an adjustment.

———

The mere fact that you adjust backbone is no indication that you have any.

———

The M. D. is well educated.
He is of the high brows.
He knows a million things not so, none of which work.
The D. C. uses common sense.
He knows one thing that is so—
will work, and works it to live and let live.

Man + operation - appendix = $100.00

Man + Chiropractic + appendix = Health

Be 100% American.

———

Keep your appendix, tonsils and other "useless organs."

———

All of which goes to prove that often the medical devil who is aggressive accomplishes more than the Doctor of Chiropractic who is passive.

———

Every time you go to a Chiropractor to get well, you get a backset.

———

There are many men who would not drown a tabby cat or let her kittens starve, who are not carrying a nickel's worth of life insurance.

———

Chiropractic is health insurance.

Premiums small. Dividends large.

———

M. D. means More Dope, More Deaths.

D. C. means Dis-ease Conquered.

———

You can no more get Chiropractic out of books than you can get to New York by reading a railroad guide.

———

Chiropractic Is Specific or It Is Nothing.

Every Person who Has Ever Been Sick Was because of a Specific Vertebral Subluxation Cause.

———

Many More Sick People Could and Should Get Well because of Intentional Specific Chiropractic Adjustment.

———

Every Person who Ever Got Well since 1895 because of Chiropractic Was because of a Specific Adjustment, whether Applied Accidentally or Intentionally, whether You Know It or not.

———

Many Sick People Have Gotten Well since 1895 without Chiropractic, but because of an Accidental Specific Chiropractic Adjustment.

———

Every Person who Has ever Gotten Well Was Because of a Specific Vertebral Subluxation Adjustment.

———

Specific Vertebral Subluxation Production and Specific Vertebral Subluxation Adjustment Were Accidental before 1895.

———

Any Method which Treats Effects Is the Practice of Medicine.

Any Method which Adjusts Vertebral Subluxation Cause Is the Practice of Chiropractic.

———

To Stimulate or Inhibit Peripheral Function Is to Practice Medicine.

To Restore Normal Transmission of Mental Impulse to Peripheral Function Is to Practice Chiropractic.

Other peoples "are different" than we Americans. But they need Chiropractic because Chiropractic is what all humanity needs.

————

God gave the ordinary Chiropractor five senses: Touch, taste, sight, smell and hearing. The extraordinary Chiropractor has two more— horse and common.

————

The human spine is composed of 26 segments, out of which medical men have composed 25,000 names for effects that radiate from it. Simplify!

————

"Evil Is to Him who Evil Thinks."
Evil Thots Are Products of Abnormal Brains.
Abnormal Brains Need Chiropractic Adjustment.
'Tis Better to Adjust Cause than Treat Effects.
Chiropractors Should Practice Rule of Cause and Effect, not Effect for Effect.

————

"Catch the Spirit of the Great Worker, B. J. Palmer, in Chiropractic. Learn to Work as He Does—Honestly, Accurately, and with Infinite Patience"   —Jordan.

————

And Some Chiropractors Want to Give a Pill as a Substitute for Innate.

What Is Chiropractic? The Practice of Doing What Comes Naturally. Define Chiropractic. To do it by hand only.

––––––

The Principal Functions of the Spine:

—to support the head

—to support the ribs

—to support the Chiropractor.

––––––

Old Therapeutical Regimes Are Failures—They Held Sway Too Long; Knowledge of Chiropractic Is Waiting to Be Tried.

––––––

The Day when a "chiropractor" Brutally Jumps from the Chandelier all up and down the Entire Backbone, to Force Multiple "adjustments," Is Past.

––––––

Puny Men Scoff at Idea of Living According to Chiropractic. They Should Try it.

––––––

Hay Made while Sun Shines Is Sown during Rains of Spring. Money Made when Chiropractor Practices Is Made when Studying at The P.S.C.

––––––

The only Thing I Have against a Chiropractor Is He Will Do to a Man's Back what He Would not Do to His Face.

––––––

The Successful Chiropractor Takes DAILY Inventory of His Thots.

Why even cabbages grow from within outward and yet many cannot understand the fundamentals of Chiropractic.

———

Get all the Chiropractic you can; can all you can get; and you will have more in your can than a physi-can can can in his can.

———

There are those who fail to grasp Chiropractic. They mix their philosophy too much with the little, insignificant self. Why then shall we wonder why they mix when their minds run foul to fundamentals?

———

You can put a whistle on a handcar and call it an engine—but it won't pull freight. Get me, some of you "Chiropractors"?

———

A chiropractor may be good, but a "specialist" can feel more important.

———

We have too many chiropractors with toes on their heels.

———

Some people are born with good teeth, some take adjustments and get them, while others have false teeth thrust upon them.

———

When FLOWING mental impulse DEcreases, STATIC dis-ease grows, health ungrows. When FLOWING mental impulse INcreases, STATIC dis-ease ungrows, health regrows. Mental impulse FLOWING in normal quantity and quality, per unit of time, IS LIFE at its best. Who knows "normal"? INNATE!

Mental impulse (1) flow, (2) matter, (3) time MUST balance to PROduce life AND health. UNbalance 1, 2, or 3—and dis-ease begins. Who knows "balance"? INNATE!

———

There Are Improvements in Everything but People. We'll Do that with Adjustments.

If ONE hammer (adjustment) will drive (correct) all kinds, sizes, and shapes of nails (dis-eases), why is it necessary (?) to give ONE HUNDRED kinds, sizes, and shapes of hammers (treatments) to drive (correct) ONE nail (dis-ease)?

———

"Nervous exhaustion"—"Nervous prostration". Why? Muscles? Nerves? Cause? Subluxation! Adjustment! Restoration!

———

Sick People Pray for Power when thru Us Would Flow a Universal Power if We Would Permit It.

———

THE FORMULA FOR FAILURE IS: TRY TO PLEASE EVERYBODY. LEONARD LYO

WE SEND A MESSAGE AROUND THE WORLD IN A SECOND AND A HALF, **BUT** IT TAKES TWENTY-FIVE YEARS TO GET AN *IDEA* THRU ONE QUARTER INCH OF SKULL.

CHARLES KETTERING

16. Medicine

Palmer's writings criticized the worldview medicine is based upon; the body is an unintelligent material machine requiring fixing. He critiqued the premise, which rests upon the notion that Educated intelligence could be more intelligent than Innate intelligence. He also called into question the hypocrisy at the core of medical practice because it did not honor the medical credo of *vis medicatrix naturae*, or 'the healing power of nature'. He wrote,

> In medicine, all acknowledge and admit that "Nature" alone cures, heals, and reestablishes health. Yet, where does medicine go to find "nature"? Inside? No, outside! Causes and cures come in bottles, teaspoons, pills, potions, drugs, operations. Obviously, we must have faith and belief in the hope that any, some, or all of these *will* cure, heal, and reestablish health and prolong life.
>
> If life and health *are inside*, it is better *to know* there is an *inside* intelligent force. When *knowledge* enters, faiths and beliefs fade out.[1]

Palmer also questions the cultural worldview, which places medicine on a pedestal. In his view, medicine was missing the primary factor in true health and healing, an acknowledgement of Innate. On this subject he wrote,

To understand ourselves, we must know our bodies and minds. To do this, we turn to THE SCIENCE of medicine. It was and is the primary study of "the existing state" of our bodies; happiness can come only as a result of its being mended better than it is now.

In THEORY, we conceded there was improvement. We saw sick surrounding us everywhere, unable to get well. We saw people healthy, get sick, and die like full-blown roses before an abnormal blasting heat.

In PRACTICE, we didn't see how it was possible that hundreds of thousands of physicians could have overlooked anything. They had millions of dollars at their command; best brains money could buy; support of 5,000 years of accumulated knowledge. They had every scientific device invented. They had been at work dissecting millions of bodies. To imagine THEY had overlooked anything important, be it immaterially large or materially small, was preposterous; hence, their library MUST have it all.[2]

Palmer was challenging the assumptions of the dominant worldview. He was not a big fan of "knocking" medicine or other health professions (although some of these epigrams seem to). He wrote,

"'Knocking' always produces a bad impression, at least it does with me, and I don't think that, in this regard, I am different from the general run of humanity."[3]

Palmer sought to add insight to the world.

Many are the Chiropractic Hoboes who desire to steal the medical unripe fruit from the legally owned farms that border the road they traverse.

———

The Chinese pay a doctor to keep them well; we Americans, an embalmer.

———

Let those who want 2 b vaccinated have it. If there is any protection in it, they have it who are vaccinated. If their own vaccination does not protect them, neither would the vaccination of the entire community.

———

Great will be the resurrection day thereof when the average woman goes to Heaven and finds that she must return to earth and gather all her parts before she can enter.

———

Physician's Association Members would go on strike if they were not afraid that the public would soon find out how to live better without them.

———

Education is a national asset. Vaccination is a national liability.

———

You and we have religious freedom granted by the Constitution of each State, and the United States. Why not Medical Freedom the same way, all the way?

———

If the "germ theory of disease" were correct, there'd be no one living to believe it.

Americans are capable of choosing their religious as well as medical methods. It's the school that is public—not the child.

————

The prescriptions are written in Latin, but the bills come to you in plain English.

————

We can choose the theology and the theologian, the politics and politician. Why not the doctor as well as the dope?

————

As a prophylactic, a hearty laugh beats 10 bottles of Peruna.

————

"Salts move the bowels"—it's the bowels which move the salts.

————

That which is natural, even tho little, is in excess of that which is artificial, even tho voluminous.

————

All that is known of anatomy is so, but all that is so of anatomy is not known.

————

What we eat and drink today goes around talking and working constructive and destructive thots and acts tomorrow.

————

Microbe Is all that Abuse, Vituperation, and Calumny Can Scientifically Be Said against Him, because the M.D. Has Telescoped and Magnascoped His every Part. You Would Die without Them; They Are Friends not Enemies; They Come to Build, not Destroy.

A license to save human life is a goat-feather a real doctor does not need, and it is something a bad doctor who cannot save human life should not have.

––––––

The M.D. disarranges man contrary to God's plan.

––––––

As citizens of the U. S. we have the intelligence to buy and sell horses and hogs; to choose the merchant with whom to do business; our wives; the mothers of our children; to pick our minister and governor; what to eat and how—yet the doctor picks our doctor; prescribes and lets us suffer; lets us live in spite of and die because of medical law; foreordains how the baby comes, how he exists and when he dies, by medical law. Is there no balm in Gilead?

––––––

Some surgeons won't take a knife in hand for less than a thousand bucks. But for that amount you can get a lot of scars that will make your friends jealous.

––––––

If you walk into a physician's office, you need a pill. If you drive up in a limousine, you need an operation.

––––––

Every time you show your tongue to the physician it costs a two-spot. It pays to keep your mouth shut.

––––––

Every organ in your body is connected with the one under your hat.

––––––

What lies ahead in health to the sick, is beyond the belief of any of us.

The by-product of the bee is more valuable in the spreading of pollen among the flowers, than the honey he makes. So is the buy-product in the relief of the sick.

———

Is it your health or your dollar the doktor works for when your appendix is worth $250.00? Sumthin's goin' to happen when you call him in!

———

Just in proportion as $250.00 is more than $2.00 is the doktor liable to advise an operation rather than an adjustment.

———

The "regular" physician knows ten thousand general things that are not so. The "specialist" knows one million specific things that are not so. Ain't it so?

———

M.D.'s write all prescriptions in Latin—otherwise we could go out in the hen yards and get it.

———

A Psychologist Is a Blind Man in a Pitch-dark Basement Looking for a Black Cat. A Psychiatrist Is a Blind Man in a Pitch-dark Basement Looking for a Black Cat that Isn't There.

———

The real difference between an ordinary doctor and a specialist is in the name and the bills.

A doctor goes to college for three years to learn how to tell you that you're not feeling well.

———

My Country 'tis of Thee
Sweet Land of Liberty
Of Thee I Sing.
Land Where My Fathers Died
Land of the Pills Inside.

———

We must defeat the efforts of those who would make sick an entire community of well people in the fear that a small portion of it may get sick.

———

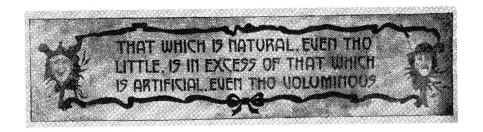

17. Common Sense

B.J. Palmer believed in common sense as the normal and natural way to access Innate as an internal flow of health and as the Innate access to genius. For Palmer, common sense was as simple as staying well. He wrote, "Does mankind WANT super education and remain sick, or the exercise of common sense and get well? Which is more important?"[1] He applied this to his concept of the Law of Life. He wrote,

> There IS and has been an INTERNAL living LAW which is and has been building and running human beings for an indefinite time on an indefinite number of people. Something INTERNAL can and does go wrong. Educated man, from OUTSIDE-IN, thinks HE is capable of "diagnosing" from OUTSIDE-IN and doing something from OUTSIDE-IN to rebuild the organ INSIDE and make it perform normally again. It would be common-sense to let THE INSIDE SOMETHING **that built that organ** and KNOWS HOW to run it, rebuild it FROM INSIDE. This CAN BE IF man admits there IS **a continuity** OF A LAW INSIDE which knows infinitely more about what, where, how and why there is an interference BETWEEN LAW INSIDE and organ INSIDE. It built it and knows how to run it and rebuild it if occasion necessitates. This single and simple law procedure would offset all EXTERNAL INTERFERENCES as complex as they are.

This LAW OF LIFE—call it by what name you think appropriate— which perpetuates itself in and thru its work and works— GIVES life **to** new born babes, and other forms of living tissues. This same law TAKES life FROM human beings, depending upon age; or, whether thru accidents or sicknesses, it alone determines the home in which IT lived is no longer inhabitable.[2]

In this quote, he equates the "boundless flow" of genius from Innate to Educated as common sense. He wrote,

Morse, Mergenthaler, Franklin, Edison, Einstein, Ford, Wright Brothers, Marconi, Tesla, Fulton, Plato, Aristotle, Euclid, Newton, D.D. Palmer...

You think they had exceptionally endowed insights, were unusually qualified, were fortunately brilliant scholars, possessed that odd and peculiar faculty called genius. Fact is, they were no different from you and me...

The ONE qualification they DID possess was a super-abundance of self-confidence in their boundless flow of common sense from ABOVE DOWN, INSIDE OUT, which is very uncommon, which makes it a rare possession, which is why so many think they possess it. Common sense makes one think clearly, reason logically, sound the depths. And drain the well from ABOVE DOWN, INSIDE OUT.[3]

Common sense is very uncommon.

―――――

The obvious is the last thing we think, see or do.

―――――

Common sense gives power to knowledge and makes wisdom in the process.

―――――

There are only a few who are possessed of common sense, that is why the masses think they have it.

―――――

Better have common sense without education than education without common sense.

―――――

We must learn right thinking as we learn to sing, for right thinking comes to us as does correct speaking—by training.

―――――

The practical man, and we dislike to give so good a name to so poor a thing, is a dogmatist, because he requires no scientific standards to prove his contentions.

―――――

Most of us suffer from illusions as the insane do. An insane person believes in things untrue. Most of us are sane on comparatively few things.

―――――

The widest road in the world is what they call the straight and narrow path.   —Sherman   Rogers,
Associate Editor "Success" Magazine, President, Optimist International

Those who are "boned up" on bookwork are no different than carrier pigeons, it still takes innate common sense to direct them home.

————

The successful progressive places more science at the command of his common sense than the "expert scientists" of their time.

————

That man is best educated who is most useful.

————

Some college "boasters" should consult Webster and learn that a Degree may mean the 360th part of a 0.

————

A Person Always Knows What to Do until It Happens to Him.

————

Why Despise a Man Because He Is a College Graduate; He May Be Long on Common Sense.

————

A Little Education Is Dangerous—It Creates Inhibitions. Too Much Education Is Equally Dangerous—It Develops Fears. Somewhere between Is Common Sense—the Self-made Man.

————

To think is labor twice distilled.

————

It's what we learn after we think we know it all, that counts.

————

Novelties and opinions shift with the wind, and people who are influenced by them are influenced by shadows.

Why State The Obvious?

————

To complex is to vex, to simplify is to amplify.
Give the man "just out" a fair chance to "stay out."

————

Many parents spend thousands on education and get a quarterback.

————

A "fool" refuses the counsel of a "wise" man, but the "wise" man often discovers truth in the speech of a "fool."

————

Life must be measured by life! Life is outside of books and colleges.

————

Many a man with horse sense refuses to say "nay."

————

Before you can do what is right, you must get the facts.

————

Conditions change, and our attitude towards them has changed, but principles remain the same.

————

Intelligence appears to be the thing that enables a man to get along without resort to education. *Education* appears to be the thing that enables a man to get alone without the use of intelligence.

————

Newly acquired knowledge is timid. It must be buttressed by experience before it becomes an integral part of the thinking equipment and before it can become the basis for sound judgment in emergencies.

Intelligence and power are attained by the absence of mental hocus-pocus.

————

The practical mystic is little concerned with incidents.

————

Everything concrete appears simple. The various qualities and elements that produce what we call mental illumination are hidden from the crowd and even from those who most profess to understand.

————

Universities are turning out hundreds of thousands of young men and young women today with brains and no sense.

—William Rainey Bennett,
Lecturer, Philosopher, and Humorist

————

We prefer to think that a dull honesty is greater than a dishonest intellectualism.

—Cecil Roberts, Editor, Novelist, Essayist, and Critic of England

————

A multitude of ignorance does not mean wisdom.

—Opie Read, Humorist, Writer, and Lecturer

————

To Believe in Miracles Is to Be Hypnotized by the Dead.

————

Some People Are Bound by Fetters of Prejudice and Superstition. They Are so Blinded They Do not Know They Are not Free, but Think Other People Are in Prison.

—Marden

There Is no "Super-natural" Power. Everything Everywhere Is the Product of Natural Law.

———

This is our program: That you and I shall base all of our thinking upon the will to know the truth; that we shall think intelligently according to an adequate number of accurate facts; that we shall think clearly, according to the laws of logical reasoning; that we shall develop the power of imagination or vision; and, lastly, that we shall base our thinking upon the unchangeable, eternal laws of the Universe.

—R. E. Pattison Kline,
Author, Lecturer, and Teacher of Effective Public Speaking

———

The Most Useful "Education" Is what We Get Thru Efforts to Make a Living.

———

Searching and Investigation of Truth Is Primary Study of Man.
—Cicero

———

Only Way One Human Being Can Influence Another Ts Encouraging Him to Think for Himself instead of Endeavoring to Instill Ready-Made Opinions.   —Sir Leslie Stephen

———

Some People Are Slow but Sure—and Some Are Just Slow.
—Ryland

———

The Poorest Way to Make up Your Mind Is to Lock It up.
—Cope

It is the Man who Doesn't Know Better who Does Things that Can't Be Done. The Fool Doesn't Know It Can't Be Done, so He Does It.

—Charles Austin Bates

————

Horse Sense Is often Developed by the Spur.

————

You LOOK with your eyes, but you SEE with mind. Odors ENTER the nose, but you SMELL with mind. Food goes INTO THE MOUTH, but you TASTE with mind. Sound enters THE EARS, but you HEAR with mind. Impressions enter ANYWHERE, but you FEEL with mind. MIND is the evaluating factor. Use it! CONCENTRATE!

————

Criticism to Be Useful, Should Rectify Errors or Improve Judgment.

————

Scientist Is One who Sees what Others Miss.

————

Education is a limitless multiplication and complexity of unnecessary necessaries.

————

Chief value of going to college is that it's only way to learn it really doesn't matter.

————

Statistics are like a Bikini bathing suit. What they reveal is suggestive but what they conceal is vital.

————

You Can Learn Anything Listening to Your Innate.

Living should be a continuous letting go of education of the past to discover greater depths in Innate's future.

––––––

You forget by reversing process of remembering.

––––––

All WE THINK we know is that WE KNOW we think that we THINK WE KNOW.

––––––

18. Friendship

True friendship is always the richest in days of greatest need.

—D.D. Palmer[1]

The highest form of friendship is a mutual resonance with total acceptance and understanding that each person is doing the best they can with the resources they have at the time. To love them no matter what, is friendship. Palmer wrote,

> There doesn't seem much good to condemn... those who disagree with our thots, because they don't know better and are doing the best they can, for what they think they know. What is beautiful to perceive is that the number of our people coming into this Innate awareness is multiplying upon itself and the numbers are reaching a point that is making the world aware THAT A NEW FACULTY IS COMING TO MANKIND AND IN TIME IT COULD BE THE NEW AGE THAT MAN IS LOOKING FOR.
>
> Our Innate and the love FLOWING THRU US FROM ABOVE-DOWN, INSIDE-OUT reaches out to each of you and in addition our gratitude and thanks are unmeasured for what you have done, not for us, but for what can be done through us in the service of others.[2]

In his classic essay on Palmer entitled, *The Man Who Made a Ladder of His Cross,* Hugh Harrison, wrote how those who "value human friendship," will value Palmer, and that he was friend to the sick. Harrison wrote,

A whole professional army has climbed up on the ladder Gen. B. J. Palmer has built out of his cross. The army is led by 20,000 lieutenants, the Chiropractic graduates. Twenty million privates—their patients—compose this vast army.

To climb to success with the good wishes of hundreds of thousands urging you still higher is inspiring. In the everlasting friendship of the sick, made well because of B. J. Palmer, he finds his greatest earthly reward. He has never unsaid his famous utterance, "Judge me by those who know my work and I will be content."

If future ages value the man who climbs with his eyes turned to the stars, if they value human friendship and service to humanity, then historians will write on bright pages the story of B. J. Palmer.

As Dr. Palmer stands on the top rung of the ladder of success today and looks back through the vista of years, years of struggle, years of relentless persecution and sleepless nights, the cross that burdened his early day is dim and indistinct. It has lost its crushing weight. He had to work to crawl out from under it. It was timber. He could not have built his ladder without it.[3]

Recipe for having friends—be one.

———

Where on earth were you yesterday?
We surely missed you!

———

A Friend Is One who Loves You and Repels Sham
Who Knows All your Faults and Doesn't Give a Damn.

———

You need us and we need you. For the things you need and we can supply, you give us the things we need and you can supply.

———

In our dealings with you, we tell you at all times the plain and simple truth, for we confess that we have lied just enough in our time to know that it won't work.

———

A good formula for forming an estimate of people is to look into our own heart.

———

Appreciation is an art—a fine art.
Some say it is a lost art.

———

Only the good can reach us, and no thot of love you send can he be lost.

———

Use your friends by being of use to them.

———

The back is that portion of your anatomy to which your "friends" direct their remarks.

When put to the test, an ounce of loyalty is worth a pound of cleverness.

———

If you want enemies, beat others to it. If you want friends, let others beat you to it.

———

Everybody thinks everybody else ungrateful. That's why we love dogs; they give us twenty dollars' worth of gratitude for ten cents' worth of dog biscuit.

———

We Have No Lukewarm "Friends." If They Understand, They're Hot. If They Misunderstand, They're Cold.

———

After Burying the Hatchet, Forget the Spot.

———

No matter how lonely you feel, Crusoe was worse. He had only Friday for company. You have the whole week.

———

It Is your Friend who Criticizes and Your Enemy Who Flatters.

———

The Man Who Is "Touching" His Friends Will Discover They Feel Cold.

———

You Get More from Enemies than from Friends. The More They Hate You the More They Advertise You.

—William Jennings Bryan

Rapidity with Which Human Mind Levels Itself to Standard Around It, Gives Most Pertinent Warning as to Company We Keep.

————

Stand with Anybody that Stands Right. Stand with Him while He Is Right and Part with Him when He Goes Wrong.

————

A Friend Is a Person with Whom We Can Think Aloud.

————

Man contends stronger for a false faith than for a true one, from the fact that truth defends itself; but a falsehood must be defended by its adherents, first to prove it to themselves, and second that they may appear right in the estimation of their friends.

————

If you lend some friends five dollars and you never see them again, it's worth it.

————

He who has a thousand friends Has not a friend to spare, And he who has an enemy Shall meet him everywhere.

————

The ornaments of a house are the friends that frequent it.

————

Friendship is based on sincerity of interest and honesty of purpose, by preference.

————

Golf clubs are all right if you can use them. Some people think the same shine about friends.

"Familiarity breeds contempt" with those who are of shadows. Familiarity breeds friendship with those who are of substance.

———

It Is easy to Tell What to Do with Bad Friends; Bother Comes in with the Good Ones Who Are no Good.

———

Any guy who knows anything about thru traffic, knows that a flagman is used to help it.

———

Quite frequently the social butterfly becomes but the fly in the social butter.

———

Some people are punctual in being late.

———

False friends are like sugar coated pills,
they soon run thru y' and leave y' much poorer.

———

United we stick,
Divided we're stuck.

———

Coming Together Is a Beginning. Keeping Together Is Progress. Working Together Is Success.

———

Dishonesty Is Suicidal. Dishonest People like Lunatics Hurt Themselves.

The Way to Cure Prejudices Is Every Man Should Let Alone Those He Complains of in Others and Examine His Own.   —John Locke

———

We Love You for What You Are and for What We Are when We Are with You.

———

When I Have Accomplished what B.J. Has Accomplished, and Overcome the Insurmountable Obstacles B.J. Has Overcome, Then I Will Be Qualified to Criticize B.J. and what He Has Done.

—Tom Morris

———

When we look at another, we see him the way Innate knows him.

———

We like others when they don't know too much.

———

People Can Be 1,000 Miles Apart and Be Close Together; and They Can Be Close Together and Be 1,000 Miles Apart.

———

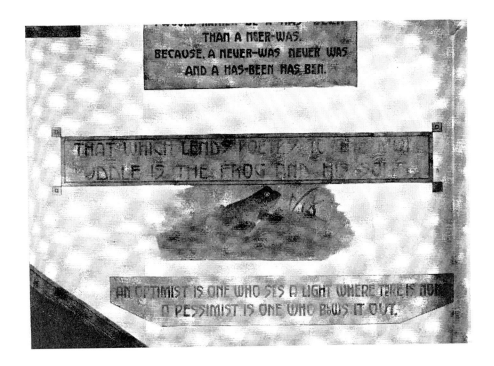

19. Social Commentary

B.J. Palmer fought for many years to make chiropractic legal and accessible everywhere. At the time of Palmer's death on May 18, 1961, there were still four states yet to legalize chiropractic; New York (1963), Massachusetts (1966), Mississippi (1973), and Louisiana (1974). Beginning with the earliest court cases, including the arrest, conviction, and imprisonment of Palmer's father in 1905 and 1906 for practicing medicine without a license, he had good reason to take a general stand for those ideas, which were unconventional and progressive. Palmer wrote,

Let an uninhibited idea come forth from the womb of the long-established centuries, tested, tried and not found wanting, out of Innate's vast storehouse, and what does inhibited educated man do to it? He hurls ridicule and sarcasm. "It can't work. What does this man know who champions it? Has he been to college? What college degrees does he have?"…

These smug, self-complacent followers of Yale, Harvard and Johns Hopkins point the finger of scorn, accuse, bring forth indictments of devious characters, try and convict the new idea in the Court of Public Opinion, of breaking down all respect for the newer order of things. Against this accusation, there is no defense. It is admitted. Convicted, the idea is sentenced to oblivion's prison. Puny man now builds a small cement and steel cell with bars at the windows and bars on the doors, thinking to imprison it and keep it from escaping into circulation.

Surrounding that unit cell, he builds a structure of organized men who form a cement and steel framework within which he tries to further incarcerate Innate's idea. And, outside of *that* structure, to make further escape impossible, he erects a huge high legislative wall, over, under or through which the idea cannot escape. On top of that legislative wall, he has high powered State Board searchlights to spot any semblance of that idea, should it try to climb the fence—each of which makes arbitrary, empirical rules and regulations. In each corner of that legislative wall he has placed basic science men with high powered rifles to shoot to kill future developments. And, if by some miracle this progressive and growing idea *should* weave back and forth through the warp and woof of these, and seemingly is going to escape, all these groups turn on the screeching sirens to notify interested bystanders to be on the watch for these dangerous escaped criminals, catch them, return them to prison, and shoot to kill if they don't surrender...[1]

A few years later, Palmer wrote,

In certain States, freedom of choice is being taken from the public in the all-important field of HEALTH....Join with us in the fight to insure your continued freedom of choice in matters affecting your health.[2]

What we suffer from in this land of the flea and home of the knave is too much "law" and too little equity.

———

We believe in freedom—social, economic, domestic, political, physical, mental, spiritual.

———

The fatal defect in all reform is over seriousness, and no reformer is sane until he can laugh at his own solemnity.

———

The people who support churches don't need them. The people who need them, can't support them.

———

"Law" is made too much for lawyers by lawyers, for we have more "law" than justice, with the consequence that Public Opinion is the only safeguard.

———

Beware of the fellow whose best reason for your doing him a favor is the fact that he belongs to the same church or lodge you do.

———

Waiting to be thanked? Hurrying to avoid the kick? Do good to others because that is the way; but if you're waiting for a receipt for your goodness you'll need a poultice. We know, for we have waited.

———

Strong convictions are often the sign of a weak intellect.

———

Have you noticed that the man who is not willing to fix himself is the one who wants the most statutes passed to fix others?

Superstition is the shadow cast by dangers long buried.

———

We need memory schools, but we also need forgettery schools more.

———

Those institutions which need endowments, can't get them. When they can get them, they won't need them.

———

Yesterday's thought is today's law.

———

Law, by its very nature, cannot keep pace with progress. It is always one day behind.

———

Progress is change.

———

The observance of the letter of the law generates cold, dogmatic thinking, and makes mere automatons of men.

———

A compromise is a device by which both parties get less than justice.

———

There must be a wise preparedness for the future; therefore, a scientific formulation of tendencies and a system of knowledge organized according to mental, spiritual and physical needs of the individual and society, so the individual may do the right thing, in the right way, at the right time, all the time.

The thinker in tune with the times is hospitable to truth; recognizes his place; knows that all is designed; respects and obeys the law as he sees its value; and changes because he sees all else change.

———

"Freak movements" always start in the minds of a few who remain for a time obscure and unknown, for all great changes of thot come from the top, from the thinkers. We call them radical, theorists and dreamers. But they make the world move because they compel the world to think.

———

The great American desert is not located in the West. It is under the hat of the average American man.

———

Education should prepare people for the duties, privileges and responsibilities in life. A smattering of Latin and Greek, mathematics and history, microscopes and telescopes, constitutes a very small portion of such equipment.

———

A person's popularity in society depends upon his P-U-R-S-E-onality.

———

That government is strongest which is weakest, and that government is weakest which is strongest.   —Gus W. Dyer,
　　　　　　　　Professor of Political Economy, Vanderbilt University

———

You can't make a nation strong by compulsion brought to bear on the individual.   —Gus W. Dyer,
　　　　　　　　Professor of Political Economy, Vanderbilt University

The life of every individual, institution and nation is a ledger. On the credit side are Rights, Privileges and Prerogatives. On the debit side are Duties, Obligations and Responsibilities.

———

To compromise with anything medical in legislation, is to accept something short of full freedom which would be part of slavery.

———

What we call civilization is a demonstration of man's energy, largely of his selfishness, partly of his intelligence.

———

The Latin verb "succedere" means to follow. Cedere means to give in. If you want to be a "success" you must follow, give in, conform.

———

No man has the right to do that, the doing of which by all, would defeat the purpose for which the organization exists.

———

Now this is the law of the jungle—as old and as true as the sky. And the wolf that shall keep it may prosper, but the wolf that shall break it must die. As the creeper that girdles the tree-trunk, the law runneth forth and back; For the strength of the pack is the wolf, and the strength of the wolf is the pack. Now these are the laws of the jungle, and many and mighty are they; But the head and the hoof of the law, and the haunch and the hump is—Obey!

———

The undertaker is, at times, a real friend of human progress.

The chief motive of a college education is to escape actual participation in just such work as gives joy to the worker.

———

Why should a university perpetuate a revolt against Innate in which the man who does no useful work is considered a gentleman and the man who by his labor feeds and clothes the world, adds to its comfort, health, efficiency and wealth and beauty, is considered low caste?

———

In China the idle idolize the idol.
In America the idle idolize the idle.

———

We have spent our time making scientific ministers, lawyers and doctors out of men and now find it necessary to face about and make human and humane men out of doctors, lawyers and ministers.

———

When a man is qualified, sincere, and not afraid to work, humanity profits.

———

The acid test of education is what it PRODUCES.

———

Too much "science" and not enough conscience. The whole basis of living, legal, ethical and educational service is the ten commandments.

———

Our school system, from kindergarten to university, appears to be designed to prepare the student for hog competition.

———

Never take fate in your own hands. It crushes you if you do.

Duz it show good sense to put peepul in charge of the Public Health who make their livin' off'n sick peepul? The doktor or undertaker least of all.

———

A community can thrive only when all its classes feel that they have common interests.

———

If a man violates man's law, we send him to prison and point the finger of scorn at him. If he violates nature's laws, we take him to the hospital and send him flowers.

———

The master preacher took people just as he found them and tried to help them to be better.

———

Some people would never think of stealing a cent from a fellowman, but it is different if they can beat the railroad or the government.

———

The closer people huddle together in cities the farther apart they get.

———

There is more religion in some men's science than there is science in some men's religion.

———

If some sermons were as broad as they are long, we would be better off.

———

A "specialist" is one who knows more and more about less and less.

A famous man is principally remembered at two times, while he is alive. 1st, when the mass want to throw something. 2nd, when they want to borrow something.

————

Men receive their gifts when they come into the world. Some think they come from those in power.

————

History has been made by "law-breakers."
Few "law-breakers," however, have made history.

————

You break the Ten Commandments—in their spirit—and the Ten Commandments will break you—in your flesh.

————

Every great institution is the lengthened shadow of a *married* man.
—Elbert Hubbard, nee B. J.

————

Science will never be happy until it can lay an egg.

————

A college education never hurt anybody who was willing to learn something afterward.

————

A man will love a dog of any color or breed, Yet, hate his fellowman because of color or creed.   —Charles Reilly

————

Narrow doctrine restricted creed, Make hungry souls on prejudice feed.   —Charles Reilly

Culture Cannot Make Character, but Character Gives Culture.

————

To make certain crime doesn't pay, Government should try it.

————

Nothing defies the law of gravity except taxes.
Income tax—the fine for successful thriving.

————

Middle-aged people usually disapprove of things. They don't like this or that. Most of them have tight corsets on ideas which are prisoners peering out cautiously from behind bars of egotism, fear or hypocrisy.

————

In the Old Days the Man Who Saved Was a Miser; Nowadays He Is a Wonder.

————

One Tree Can Make a Million Matches. One Match Can Burn One Million Trees. It Takes One Tree Fifty Years to Grow. It Takes One Match One Day to Burn the Tree. Moral: Some People Grow Trees; Others Burn Them.

————

20. Work

Palmer was tireless in his quest to bring health and enlightenment to a sick a world. He constantly pushed himself and the profession, sometimes creating conflict along the way. In 1924, he introduced a new technology into the profession, thermography, to objectively measure the vertebral subluxation. The new device was expensive and he wanted all chiropractors to use it. This led to a break with his core faculty who started their own school. The pressure was so much for Palmer, he checked into a sanitarium for a short time, eventually healing himself by building an extraordinary garden, with waterfalls, statues, and rocks. Palmer wrote,

Some men are wise beyond their years or environment. Same man could be and sometimes is pound wise and ton foolish. He is much like a car—some race at 138 miles per hour, others drag along until they wear out.

We recall a time when, for 18 consecutive years, we worked 365 days, 18 hours per day; then the machine wore out and refused to run. We were shipped to Pass Christian, Mississippi. They sent a court reporter with us because we refused to budge unless they did. Each day they hauled us out on a cot over a long fishing pier into the gulf, where there was a covered house. It was there we dictated 100,000 words a day, flat on our back.

It did not take us long to regain our spizzerinctum.[1]

Soon after that incident, Palmer traveled the world three times, opened the radio station, introduced his upper cervical specific technique, and opened a million dollar research clinic, and eventually wrote about twenty more books. His mission was clearer than ever and he was not to slow down again for some time. He wrote,

We concede to rest physically one day of the week is good; but to tell us not to work or we will be damned, then we refuse the accusation. At one time man was jailed for selling bread on sabbath—he broke a religious commandment. God builds vegetables, animals, even the child in uterus on Sunday, as conscientiously as any other day. He who labors to improve mankind mentally or physically, thereby making better the spiritual on SUNDAY, is a God-like man and fulfilling the commandment to "Remember to keep holy the Sabbath day." Is not EVERY DAY a God's day? Why not remember to keep the WEEK DAY holy? Do nothing on a week day you wouldn't do on Sunday. Are we an infidel, agnostic, or atheist because our Sabbath is six-times greater than yours?[2]

Work is life. Good work is good life.

―――――

Pick up thy load and work.

―――――

Concentrate upon the work in hand. The sun's rays do not burn until brought to a focus.

―――――

We think if we worked for a man, we would work for him. We would not work for him a part of his time, but all of his time. We would give an undivided service or none.

―――――

Blessed is the man who has found his work.

―――――

By the telephone exchange, where people do love to linger and chin, chat and chew and say much of sweet nothings, we have this one:

One of our greatest assets—talk, we work overtime, most of us.

―――――

Head, Heart and Hand!

―――――

You are not dressed for work until you put on a smile.

―――――

We choose our helpers by the amount of work they do, with the least supervision, in the best and easiest way, in the shortest possible time.

―――――

You push your business,
Then let your business push you.

A hen is the only living critter that can set still and produce dividends.

———

The woodpecker is a knocker, but he uses his head; and that's what it takes to get the worm.

———

It takes 65 muscles to frown and 13 to make a smile. Why work overtime?

———

And when the Great Cashier comes to enter a Credit, Thon will write not how much, but what you gave to get it.

———

Cast your bread upon the workers and it will return sandwiches.

———

Ab-so-lute-ly!

———

The world is your cow—
But you must do the milking.

———

Whatever your job is, it is your job.

———

The employer who pays his helpmates less than they are worth, or treats them as other than human beings, may be unjust and a criminal; but, that "helper" who accepts pay for hours he does not deliver, poses as a craftsman and delivers shoddy work and is careless with materials because his "boss is rich" is related to a thief, obtains money under false pretenses and also deserves his full measure of condemnation.

The sweetness of low prices can never counterbalance the bitterness of poor quality.

―――――

Rest is the sweet sauce of labor.

―――――

Art is the expression of a man's joy in his work. You must let the man work with his head, heart and hand, and then out of the joy beauty will be born.

―――――

We are not here to play, to dream, to drift; we have hard work to do and loads to lift. Shun not the struggle, face it, 'tis God's gift.

―――――

We believe in working, not weeping; in boosting, not knocking; and in the pleasure of our job.

―――――

Folks who never do more than they get paid for, never get paid for more than they do.

―――――

We believe that a man gets just what he goes after; that one deed done today is worth two deeds tomorrow; and that no man is down and out until he has lost faith in himself.

―――――

We believe in today and the work we are doing―in tomorrow and the work we hope to do, and in the reward which the future holds.

―――――

Remember―"I forgot" won't do in business.

Three classes of people are entitled to indulge in indulgence—invalids, prisoners and lunatics.

———

R U Busy?

———

The rolling stone gathers no moss, but it gains a damn fine polish.

———

Socialists declare that the day is coming when the aristocracy will have to work. We foresee a time when even the working-classes will have to work.

———

Refuse to be a sand-bar.

———

If the employer of labor thot work to do on a union scale of hours, with the union degree of effort and with the union loss of time and survival values, Lord pity the employee. A union five minutes per day would do it all.

———

The union man who talks about the "right of Labor" as something different from the rights of anyone else, scorns efficiency because he wants to make work for as many as he can, at as big wages as he can, without reference to production or cooperation.

———

You never hear the busy man complaining about his lot in life. It's always the loafer.

The teacher, the preacher, or anyone else who gets on the retired list, retires himself.

———

Only the hen can earn money by laying around.

———

Tell the lobscouse loafer who has tempus to incinerate who comes, hesitates, stays and gabfests, that WE HAVE WORK TO DO—AND SO HAVE YOU.

———

Safety First.

———

Women continue to attend bargain sales, and men keep on buying oil stock, but the question of getting "something for nothing" remains unanswered.

———

The cure of poverty is in better production.

———

An hour of worry is more exhausting than a day of Hard Work.

———

The fellow who is fired with enthusiasm for his work is seldom fired by his boss.

———

While working for money, make money work for you.

———

Many Men Find What They Want to Do after They Have Done Most Things Wrongly.

Work thou for pleasure.
Paint or sing or carve
The thing thou lovest,
Though the body starve.
Who works for glory
Misses oft the goal,
Who works for money
Coins his very soul.
Work for the work's sake,

———

Give us this day our chance to work and earn our bread.

———

When We Work, There Is Fun Loafing.

———

Happiness Is a By-product Obtained from Work Well Done.

———

Every Noble Life Leaves its Fibre Interwoven in Work of the World.
—John Ruskin

———

One Reason Why the Dollar Will Not Do as Much as It Used to Is that Many People Do Not Want to Do as Much for a Dollar as They Used to.

———

What we do willingly, is a pleasure. What we do begrudgingly, is hard work.

Man Who Gets in on Ground Floor Usually Stays there.

———

Work faithfully 8 hours. Don't worry. In time you will become the executive and work 18 hours a day and do all the worrying.

———

The Man who Would Rise beyond Time Clock Can Afford to Forget It.

———

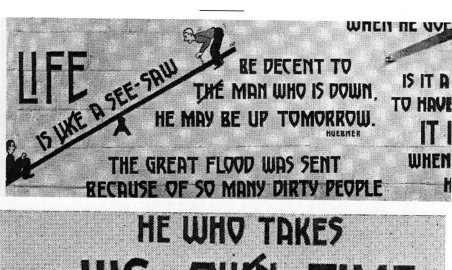

70. In A Little Bit O' Heaven. Italian bronze statue. Waterfalls.

21. Communication

Communication was one of Palmer's greatest strengths. This quote gives us some insight into his process of fine tuning his message. Palmer wrote,

> We then write whatever comes, as it comes, be it good or bad. We keep writing as long as thoughts flow, and they always flow without effort. We may knock out some, much, or all of it later. Much of this may be out of sequence. We keep on until the present line of thinking is exhausted. Then we let it simmer and settle for an hour, hours, days, or weeks. Usually, when building a lecture, it is more or less steadily on our minds, and we are constantly harassed by Innate to keep on keeping on whipping it into shape. Usually, in a few days or a week or two, it is finished for the time being. Soon a new line of thinking may begin to flow, and away goes the typewriter again. We frequently rewrite our copy the second or third time before we get it to say exactly what we mean... Altogether, one lecture may represent scores or hundreds of hours from time of conception to laying it away to rest. That's the process we use in *building* a lecture.[1]

In Palmer's view one must first learn to listen to Innate. He wrote,

> Clearest, best of Innate's vast wisdom thought-flashes come through at night. Innate is so often insistent that this youngster many and many a

time found his nights consistently awakened with his most brilliant solutions of the most bothersome problems.

What usually happens to the average person WHO WANTS TO KNOW HOW TO RECEIVE INNATE'S THOUGHT-FLASHES? In daytime, you get them and pass by them. At night, you are relaxed, asleep, education is blanked out. Quietly and easily, Innate has a solution for some problem which worried education. Innate flashes through to your NOW empty educated brain; it awakens education; you begin to get ready to commence to think YOU had a solution.

Silently, Innate sneaks up on your sleepy self. Innate flashes answers so you MAY have them. Instead of getting up, having a pad and pencil handy alongside your bed, writing while the idea is in full clarity, you roll over on the other side, education saying, "I'll remember that tomorrow and then I'll think able about it and if it is worth while will write it." Right THERE AND THEN you made your big mistake! In the morning, education is top man again. Innate is back in its retreat, doing only these things which it has to do to keep physical functions in motion. You didn't CAPTURE that idea when Innate WANTED TO AND WAS WILLING TO GIVE; so you educationally lost it. The more this indifference occurs this way, the more Innate becomes discouraged and eventually ignores YOU because YOU ignored Innate, until it becomes a fixed habit both ways, each ignoring the other.[2]

Be sure you're right—then force the fight.

————

What to say, how to say it, and when.

————

Tact is the science of knowing how to get what you want and don't deserve, from a bigger man, without getting hurt.

————

If you are in the right, you can afford to keep your temper. If you are in the wrong, you cannot afford to lose it.

————

Keep your feet warm and your head cool, is a pretty good rule. "Hot heads" always go with "cold feet."

————

We would rather be "up" on a "live" Yankee talk than "down" into "roots" of a "dead" Latin or Greek.

————

Men are born with two eyes but with one tongue, in order that they may see twice as much as they say.

————

Evidence is not a statement of truth, but a proof of the truth of a statement.

————

The Lincoln-Douglas debate was a direct collision of two opposing forces or viewpoints. The concussion, however, cleared the atmosphere. All saw more clearly afterward.

If eavestalkers say good of others, then eavesdroppers will hear only good of themselves.

———

It is impossible to stop people thinking. The job is to get them started.

———

The heart teaches a man what to say, but the head instructs him when to clam up.

———

Truth has always been stronger than fiction; hence, he who states it is in contradiction with the masses and he is therefore forced to produce a superabundance of proof to prove that which should be obvious.

———

A Good Listener Is Not Only Popular—He Learns Something.

———

"You have no right to try to convince us that we are wrong, for you are wrong, but we have a right to try to convince you that you are wrong *because we are right!" So* says the intolerant.

———

We Throw Mud at Living and then Plant Flowers in Mud After They Are Dead.

———

The great orator always shows a dash of indifference for the opinion of his auditors; and the great writer is he who loses self-consciousness and writes himself down as he is, for in the last analysis all literature is a confession.

Be calm in arguing, for fierceness makes error a fault and truth discourtesy.

———

He Who Excuses Himself Accuses Himself.

———

Meditate More, Talk Less, Do More.

———

A tip is not a "thank you." It is just—a tip.

———

It's o.k. to HOLD a Conversation, but It's Proper TO LET GO Now and Then.

—Richard Armour

———

Some Minds Are Like Concrete—Mixed and Set.

———

Fiction Is more of a Stranger than Truth.

———

Oratory is the art of making deep sounds from the chest seem like important messages from the brain.

———

An oration is a collection of loose words so arranged and handled that it will take them the maximum amount of time to pass a given point.

———

Orators are people who can think rapidly through the mouth.

———

The foolish are unworthy of indignation; they must be dealt with quietly but effectively; while the others must be managed with gentle firmness backed by the fundamentally drastic.

Who shall set a limit to the influence of one man? How far is his voice heard? Through him, through others, to many millions. What word, what act is it that goes on? Therefore, we should be careful of what we say, what we do, before whom we say and do it.

———

A cup of cold water, cheerfully given, should prompt a warm "thank you."

———

The employment of "thank you" is the ideal made real.

———

Of course, it is the duty of the elevator employee to carry you up and down at your command, but a "thank you" now and then, gives you a distinction above many.

———

A "thank you" is a forget-me-not from the garden of courtesy.

———

If he says, "I say just what I think," he doesn't think.

———

All too many speakers allow their tongues to make 3,000 revolutions a minute while their brains are set at neutral.

———

Radio—out of the void, into the vacuum.

———

An ounce of taffy is worth more than a pound of epi-taphy.

———

A silent man may be wise; a talker must be.

Can there be a more horrible object in existence than an eloquent man not speaking the truth?

—Carlyle

_____

Adam Was All Right When Working in the Garden. When He Stopped to Gossip He Got into Trouble.

_____

Wit and humor are shock absorbers; they are the pneumatic tires that cushion the road; they are the resilient strings that take up the jar.

—Dr. Charles Milton Newcomb, Psychologist, Author, and Humorist

_____

Profanity is a disease of the vocabulary.

—Dr. Burges Johnson, Director of Public Relations, Syracuse University

_____

One way to become conspicuous is not to write your memoirs.

_____

The English language is composed of 26 letters, out of which we have composed 514,000 words.

_____

Why freight a tub of words to express a spoon of thought?

_____

Modern writers need no more than an idea and a typewriter. In a pinch, many of them get along with the typewriter.

_____

Printers, Ink uses the pen, press and printed page.

Publicity possesses the password to power and prosperity.

Printers, Ink causes the public to pause, ponder and purchase.

Grammar is an orderly arrangement of the way certain people utter their squeaks, just as botany is an orderly arrangement of the way certain plants grow. Language preceded grammar just as flowers preceded botany. Why is a "grammar shark"?

———

Think 8 Hours, Write it in 10 Minutes, and Say it in 5.

———

We shall stop fighting words, English, grammar and rhetoric when we better learn to think.

———

All people make mistakes—that's why erasers are put on pencils.

———

If You Would Be Remembered when Dead, Write Things Worth Reading or Read Things Worth Writing.   —Benjamin Franklin

———

Some Writings, Like Some Streams, Appear Deep when They Are merely Muddy.   —Elbert Hubbard

———

Think straight, talk straight, and you will be thought straight.

———

The little lady at the switchboard occasionally may slip a cog and give you the wrong number, but it's a ten-to-one shot that she expedites service, just the same. The big thing for you to do is to say "thank you" once in a while to let other folks know that it's in you.

———

Diplomacy Is to Say the Nastiest Things in the Nicest Way.

A classical journal once compiled what purported to be "the one hundred most inspiring words in the English language." They follow: Almighty, achievement, ambition, aspiration, beautiful, chivalry, confidence, consecration, courage, determination, devotion, earnestness, efficiency, enterprising, enthusiasm, faith, fame, fortitude, friendship, happiness, heroism, home, hope, ideal, illustrious, indomitable, invincible, justice, knowledge, liberty, loyalty, magnanimous, mercy, mother, peace, perseverance, progress, righteousness, sympathy, thanksgiving, truth, virtue, will, youth, zeal.

———

If you would be a man speak what you think today in words as hard as cannon balls, and tomorrow speak what tomorrow thinks in hard words again even tho it contradicts everything you said today.

———

Sincerity alone, therefore, is not enough; it must be wise or it may be diabolical.

———

Kiss is a noun, generally used as a conjunction. It is never declined; it is not singular, and it is usually used in the plural.

———

The world is large enuf for men with differences of opinion but life is too short to be enemies because thereof.

———

The feller that agrees with everything you say is either a nut or he is gettin' ready to skin you.

———

First, Man Talks. After Years, He Learns to Think.

To quote Emerson, "What you are speaks so loudly, I cannot hear what you say."   —William K. Braasch,

———

Man's Mouth Is Too Little for His Thots.

Silence Your Opponent with Reason—not with Noise.

—Hale

———

We Send a Message Around the World in a Second and a Half, but It Takes Twenty-five Years to Get an Idea Thru One-Quarter Inch of Skull.   —Kettering

———

Courtesy and Composure Are Weapons of Life; They Make Us Superior to Opponents When They Storm Us.   —Robert Bersuny

———

Many Have Suffered by Talking, but Few by Silence.

———

Reform Those Things in Yourself You Blame in Others.

———

Virtue Never Needs Vociferation.

———

Such as Boast Much, Usually Fail Much.

———

Some People Think with Brains. That Is a Quiet Process. Others Think with Mouths, Irishmen with Fists, and Mules with Feet.

———

Why Give Advice? Wise Men Have Their Own and Fools Avoid It.

Man Who Can Bottle His Wrath Is a Corker.

———

More a Man Talks on a Subject, More Good It Would Do Him to Think on it.

———

"Tell a Lie often Enuf, long Enuf, and strong Enuf, and People Will Believe It."   —Nugent (Hitler said that, too.)

———

For a lie which is a half truth Is ever the greatest of lies, Since a lie which is all a lie May be met and fought outright, But a lie which is a part truth, Is the harder to fight.

                        —Tennyson (How well Murphy and Nugent use this.)

———

When Man Hears Himself Misrepresented It Provokes Him. When Misrepresentation Becomes Gross and Palpable It Is Apt to Amuse Him.

———

Rage Robs a Man of Reason and Makes Him a Laughing Stock.

———

Silence Is more Significant than most Expressive Eloquence.

———

Heated conversation may make an office warm, but never comfortable.

———

We like people who keep their word, temper and friends.

———

Half truth is often a total lie.

———

Kind word dropped today will bear fruit tomorrow.

Difference between right word and almost-right word is difference between lightning and lightning bug.

———

A speaker is finished when he sits down.

———

To say the right thing at the right time, keep still most of the time.

———

In deluding loneliness of living within a human skull and not being able to penetrate neighboring skulls with any proof of certainty, we try to speak the theme aloud.

———

One tragedy of this age-old search for health is that words have become shiny from handling; meaning has rubbed off. They must be re-forged in our own desperate fire.

———

Most thinking we think we do isn't a monologue—it's a dialogue.

———

Man you speak to silently will answer you openly.

———

Thank-U-Grams are free—as are all best things in life.

———

Long and slow is education. Not weeks, months, or years, but generations for man to speak across miles and customs to touch other men's minds enough to change them permanently into better habits of health, living, and thinking.

A Popular Person Gives His CANDIED Opinion.

———

People sensible enough to give sound advice are usually sensible enuf to give none.

———

His Mouth Often Works Faster than His Brain—He Says Things He Hasn't Thot of.

———

Automobiles Do Not Run Down as Many People as Gossip.

———

Some People, like Boats, Toot Loudest when They're in a Fog.

———

Wise Man Flatters the Fool. Fool Flatters Himself.   —Loth

———

Every Innate man is a library, if you know how to read him.

22. Greatness & Leadership

Following from previous chapters, Palmer expands on the possibility of contacting Innate for each person. He compares such access to an opening of the volcanic flood gates. This process is transformative and points to a potential for greatness and leadership in all people. Palmer wrote,

> He who composes, invents, writes, inspires, enjoys his work because it is an unfolding process from within.
>
> From whence came the music of the musicians, the ideas of inventions, the writings of writers? Every one opened the flood gates of that which was within himself and let it flow outward.
>
> The Innate within each of us is the sum total of Westinghouse, Tesla, Marconi, Edison, Steinmetz, Beethoven, Mozart, Haydn, Irving Berlin, D. D. Palmer—and more. Innate is everything to everybody. It is all that everybody has been; has thought, said, written, or printed. Innate is everybody who lives. You, too, are living. The potentials are there. They may be dormant, but they can be active. Unlock any door you prefer, it is yours for knowing how. Any man, if he knows how, can open any room of his Innate. Any man can do what others have done...
>
> *The potential is in you.* It lies dormant, inactive, like a smoldering volcano choking back its pent-up fires, ready to burst forth as soon as a natural opening is made possible. ... Is there a something, a force, a

factor, a power, a science, a knowledge— call it what you will—which a few people understand and use to overcome their difficulties and achieve outstanding success? I firmly know there is, and it is my desire to explain it so that you may use it if you desire.[1]

And yet, even more than his admonishment to be one of the great ones, Palmer opens the possibility that this is a source of spiritual advancement, a way to commune with the infinite by tapping the gateway, the source. He wrote,

Some few men possess the INNER "AWARENESS" to let THE INNER GREATER intellectuality come thru to the lesser, darker outer fellow and shed its "light." Even THEY do not fully comprehend HOW they tapped the gateway source of infinity knowledge and ability.[2]

Palmer even claims that this is what the great spiritual teachers have done,

This being a truism—that the Innate pattern of ALL people IS fixed, stable, internally-eternal, and is alike in all—then each educated person has the same right to turn on the internal faucet BETWEEN Innate IN him and permit it to flow into his Educated, the same as the Christ, Buddha, Therese, Shogni, Helen, Pope Pius, Albert, or any other individual…[3]

Some seek greatness, some acquire it, and some have greatness thrust upon them.

———

One great, strong, unselfish soul in every community would actually redeem the world.

———

We can't all be leaders, but there's a lot that goes with showing 'em actual worth.

———

Produce great persons—the rest follows.

———

A man is clean outside and in; he neither looks up to the rich nor down to the poor; he can lose without squealing and win without bragging; he is considerate of women, children, and old people; he is too brave to lie, too generous to cheat, and he takes his share of the world and lets others have theirs.

———

With public sentiment nothing can fail. Without public sentiment, nothing can succeed. Consequently, he who moulds public sentiment goes deeper than he who enacts statutes or pronounces decisions.

———

With God thy father, man thy brother, Oh, be thyself a man. Each for himself, yet for each other Is God's eternal plan.

———

Great principles, like great men, are simple.

After reaching fame, many a climber has found it an uncomfortable roost.

————

Over Elevator:

There's plenty of room on top,

The only way is by climbing—

Most people are waiting for the elevator here below.

————

A man's a man for a' that, but lots of them are not even that.

————

Kites fly against the wind, not with it.

————

A winner never quits. A quitter never wins.

————

Men whom people call crazy today, they build wonderful monuments to, tomorrow.

————

As we so solve and dissolve our own problems, the world is drawn to us to solve its problems. We find our kitchen, workshop or office becoming a new throne of power.

————

Of course the lions didn't eat Daniel—he was all backbone.

————

Responsibilities gravitate to the person who can shoulder them, and power flows to the man who knows how.

————

In your lap rocks the destiny of the world.

Vision—the driving force that impels every great organization. Egotism—the badge of ignorance. Confidence—the symbol of knowledge.

———

A few men who possess antiquated power, legal power and selfish ambition have dragged the others along, raising us gradually to what is called education.

———

In America we need men who have the courage to break, to contradict, resist, criticize, be unpopular. We need less "successes" and more "failures"—men who may bestow imperishable gifts.

———

Make your decision for what is RIGHT, not expedient, and wash your mind of all compromise.

———

To be great is to be misunderstood.

———

Who Can Dispose of a Great Man by Traducing Him?
Who Can Get Rid of a Great Question by Ignoring It?
Who Can Thwart a Great Cause by Misrepresenting It?

—Dr. W. C. Abbott

———

The Man Worthy of Being a Leader never Complains of Stupidity of Helpers, of Ingratitude of Mankind, nor of Inappreciation of Public. These Are a Part of the Game of Life. To Meet Them and Stay on Top of Discouragement and Defeat Is Final Proof of Power.

—Elbert Hubbard

We spend half our time crying for great leadership, and the other half crucifying great leaders when we are lucky enough to find them.

—Dr. Glenn Frank, President University of Wisconsin

———

A vigorous and curbed temper is not altogether an evil. Men who are easy as an old shoe are generally of as little worth.

———

Greatness always appeals to the future.

———

The mark of a man of the world is absence of pretension. He does not make a speech, he takes a low tone, avoids all brag, promises not at all, performs much.

———

Shake hands with the man who is agreeable enough to encourage you in your thinking and disagreeable enough to make you think harder.

———

All some people do is to second the motion.

———

When any man reaches the position where his opinion is valuable, it is the laughing gas Fate lets him sniff when She means to strike him on the head.

———

It is a 100 to 1 shot that if you know any man who has become famous, you know the man who got just about the worst the world could give him before his light went out.

Is a man dead if his ideals live?

———

The great man is the harmonious combination of what is particular with what is general.

———

To Be in Line Is Good. To Lead Is Better.

———

Little Deeds Are Like Little Windows in a Large Room.

———

Some People Remind Me of Fractions—the Bigger They Try to Be, the Smaller They Are.

———

As Ego Expands, Brain Contracts.

———

Keep Your Head Cool—Feet Warm—Mind Busy. Plan Work Ahead and Stick to It—Rain or Shine. If You Are a Gem, Someone Will Find You.

———

If There Is Anything the World Hates More than a Quitter, It Is the Man Who Refuses to Quit when He Is Through.   —Lippincott

———

The Man Who Is "up in the Air" Seldom Occupies a Lofty Position.

———

Great Minds Are Easy in Prosperity and Quiet in Adversity.

———

Fellow Who Thinks His Job Is Unimportant Usually Gets that Kind.

The Art of Commanding Is to Take a Fair Share of Work.

—Noah Porter

———

I Wonder to See Men Wicked; but I Wonder to See Them not Ashamed.   —Dean Swift

———

Courage Consists in Blindly Overlooking Danger and in Meeting It with Eyes Open.   —Richter

———

Fame Comes when Deserved, and then Is as Inevitable as Destiny for It Is Destiny.   —Longfellow

———

We Love the Rooster for Two Things—the Crow that Is in Him, and Spurs that Are on Him to Back up the Crow.

———

The Brave and Bold Persist Against Fortune; the Timid and Cowardly Rush to Despair thru Fear.

———

The Heights of Great Men Reached and Kept
Were Attained by Slow Flight,
But They, While Their Companions Slept,
Were Toiling Upward in the Night.

—Longfellow

———

As Small Letters Hurt Sight, so Do Small Matters Hurt Him Who Is Intent upon Them.   —Plutarch

State Facts of an Original Idea. There Are Enough Imitators and Commonplace Individuals without You.

———

Horses Get Nowhere until Harnessed. Steam and Gas Get Nowhere until Confined. Niagara Is Turned into Light and Power when Tunneled. Life Grows Great when It Is Focused, Dedicated to a Great Principle, and Disciplined in Action.   —Harry Emerson Fosdick

———

Masses Fear Laughter, Scoffs, and Jibes, Forgetting that Men Who Have Done Great Work thru Ages Have Received much Pay in Laughter, Scoffs, and Jibes.   —from the Ignorant

———

Censure Is a Tax which those who Fill Situations Expect to Pay.

———

World Belongs to the Enthusiast who Keeps Cool.

———

It is easy to dodge responsibilities, but we cannot dodge consequences of dodging responsibilities.

———

So live that when you die undertaker will be sorry.

———

Every man living can do more than he thinks he can—IF he THINKS he can!

———

Where there is no vision, the people perish.
                —Proverbs 29:18

9. In the home of author. North wall of Music Room. Pipe organ manual below.
Oil painting of B.J. by Raymond P. R. Neilson.

23. Service

Service was at the center of Palmer's life and actions. He viewed his life a vessel for something much greater than he. He even came to call himself We. The vision he held and the ability to gather like-minded visionaries taking massive action was destined to change the world for millions. He wrote,

We are merely the office holder of an international trust born into us by our father, and early we found ourself ENTIRELY INADEQUATE TO HANDLE THE JOB; WE FOUND OURSELF TOO SMALL and of too small an intellect to carry this movement of pushing Chiropractic to the front. The job was too big for us to swing; our capabilities were limited; our experience beggardly; our resources small; our mental capacity shallow; our business opportunities too circumscribed for our vision of service.

At the end of a year or two, many years ago, we found ourself with a mountain on our hands and a teaspoon with which to move it; an international movement of service to the human race, with one small feeble body to carry it; a great, big, inward surging and propelling motive to save a sick world, with a bankrupt mind and untrained hands to do it.

It IS true we felt the great, big, inward urge and had a young incompetent outward shell with which to do it. There was but ONE thing to do, viz., SURROUND OURSELF WITH MEN WHO COULD, WOULD AND DID GET OUR VISION and thus MULTIPLY OUR USEFULNESS BY MULTIPLYING MEN WHO COULD HELP. So, we have been gathering those big men.[1]

Palmer viewed his actions, his service, and his life in the context of hundreds if not thousands of years in the past and future. He sought to share his truth with as many people in as many forms as possible. It is lucky for us, he dedicated so much time to writing. His legacy of service is for the future to interpret. Palmer wrote,

If what we say IS expressive of basic reality, which none can dispute or deny, it matters not what may be said against it or how some chiropractors cast it lightly to one side, it will live and some day have its rightful place in a better service to mankind.[2]

The final quote from Palmer's last years of life is reproduced at the end of this chapter. It sums up much of what these introductions describe, a capacity, inherent in all, not always available, as he mentions above, yet one which can be learned, cultivated, and harnessed for consistent and constant access and flow in service, in love, and in bigness.

The Infinite is not a bankrupt and we who represent the Infinite should not be. If we wish to be of service to others we must have power, but to get it we must give it; we must be of service.

———

Put Serve in your service and omit the ice.

———

Strike while the iron is heated, Pause, and the iron's cold; If you strike too late on a hardened plate, The weld will never hold.

Seek, and success will follow; Wait, and it passes by; Be quick to grasp, then hold it fast, and work for a better day.

Serve and the world serves with you; Loaf, and you loaf alone; This strenuous world is a continuous whirl—It offers no room for the drone.

———

We believe in the stuff we are handing out; in the firm we are working for; and in our ability to get results. We believe that honest stuff can be passed out to honest men by honest methods.

———

Crookedness never pays in the long run. Look at the corkscrew—now it's out of a job.

———

Christ went about healing the sick. Be a Christian and the heathen is upon you.

———

Service to others is enlightened self-interest.

One good deed leads to another. One evil deed leads to another. The law is irrevocable. They are in groups and none can occur without the whole. On every deed there is a tax and the tax must be paid. It is the law.

———

Many men resent being awakened; they like the morning nap with its vague dreaming, when the world is neither wholly present nor wholly absent.

———

Americans of today won't "pass the buck."

———

Our duty is to be useful, not according to our desires but according to our powers.

———

There isn't much salvation in being able to quote the Bible unless there is application to go with it.

———

We make a living by what we get; but a life by what we give.

———

The evil men do lives after them; so does the good.

———

Some people are like sponges; they take unto themselves all they possibly can hold, but give nothing unless squeezed.

———

The ideal preacher is more interested in getting heaven into men than in getting men into heaven; and in keeping hell out of men than in keeping men out of hell.

It is good to be great, but it is great to be good.

———

To be wealthy is no crime; but to have wealth and do no good with it is a crime.

———

Men are vastly more interested in a religion of service than in a religion of services.

———

A man does not have to be full of conviction to make a moral noise, nor a radiator full of steam to granule.

———

If you are trying to help people in the mass, you must allow for human imperfections.

———

When we do good, we feel good; When we do bad, we feel bad, And that's our religion.

———

Any law of compensation where service is eliminated, is a speculation and a game of chance.

———

No One Is Useless in the World Who Lightens the Burdens of It for Anyone Else.   —Charles Dickens

———

Men exist for the sake of one another. Teach them, then, or bear with them.

We Have no More Right to Consume Happiness without Producing It, than to Consume Wealth without Creating It.

—George Bernard Shaw

———

Do All the Good You Can and Make as Little Fuss as Possible.

—Charles Dickens

———

It Requires More Brains and Greater Courage to Practice Golden Rule than Win Battles. Measure Stars or Gain Wealth.

———

To Get What You Seek and Have no Other Objective Is to Drink of the Dregs of Misery.

———

Be Good, but Be Good for Something.

—Henry David Thoreau

———

If You Are on the Highway to Success, Show Others the Way and You'll Have Company. Some Men who Attained Success Are Lonesome.

———

Get—to Give.
Give—to Get.

———

There Are no Innocent Bystanders when Injustice Is Done.

———

Golden Rule Is Best Antidote for Rule of Gold.

Fault finding requires no talent; no self-denial, no brains, no character are required to set up in the grumbling business.

———

It Is as Much YOUR Fight to GET as It Is OUR Fight to GIVE.

———

He profits most who serves best.—Rotary.

He serves best who profits most.—Palmer.

It makes a paradox.

———

To Give and to Lose Is Nothing; but to Lose and to Still Give Is the Part of a Great Mind.   —Seneca

———

Greatest Man Is Greatest Servant.

———

Growing is always into, not away from.

———

We Never Know How Far Reaching Something We May Think, Say, or Do Today Will Affect the Lives of Millions Tomorrow.

CAPACITY

EVERY person HAS latent or dormant potential CAPACITIES.

—Some call them "intuitions, hunches"

—Others call them thot-flashes or inspirations

—Some have Innate CAPACITY and don't know it

—Some have Innate CAPACITY and deny its existence

—Some have Innate CAPACITY and ignore its presence

—Some have Innate CAPACITY and deplore it

—Some have Innate CAPACITY and are too lazy to develop it

—Some have Innate CAPACITY and refuse to explore it

—Some have Innate CAPACITY and refuse to listen

—Some have Innate CAPACITY and call it a "cult"

—Some have Innate CAPACITY and need be trained, like robots, to use it

—Some have Innate CAPACITY and use it constantly

—Some have Innate CAPACITY and work with it consistently

That's why SOME succeed and others fail to be all they could be.

"CAPACITY"—That internal unexplored depth, which when brot to the surface makes each person bigger, better, stronger, more capable to carry the load of improved service to his fellow men…

We do want you to know WE LOVE YOU BECAUSE YOU LOVE ALL THINGS WE LOVE. To us, you are like a great big bubbling-over enthusiastic family, in mischief one minute, and saving the world by adjusting vertebral subluxations the next.

For, we never know how far-reaching something we may think, say or do today will affect the lives of millions tomorrow.

GET THE IDEA, ALL ELSE FOLLOWS.

Epilogue
B.J.Palmer
An Integral Biography

This epilogue examines B.J. Palmer's life using the Integral model as developed by philosopher Ken Wilber. Known as Integral Theory, the framework has been applied to dozens of disciplines, from personal growth to politics, psychology to science, economics to subtle energies, and consciousness studies to ecology. This article applies Integral Theory to biography. Integral biography is a way to examine an individual's life while including the increasing levels of complexity that develop through cultural, social, subjective, and behavioral domains. In this regard, the epilogue's's goal is twofold: 1) to describe B.J. Palmer's life through the integral lens, and 2) to map out some important aspects of *integral biography*, a new approach to biography.

Joshua Bartlett "B.J." Palmer (1882-1961) was a 20th century integral pioneer—he developed, in his own consciousness, a comprehensive way of thinking and being in the world, embodying a de-centered ego, an integration of body, mind, and spirit, a holistic or systems worldview, and a presence and vision that impacted many. To suggest Palmer reached this stage towards the end of his life does not ignore his faults, interpersonal challenges, or suggest his development was complete, only that his final days were characterized by the integral perspective. The integral level of consciousness has been researched and written about extensively in terms of ongoing adult development across several lines, such as values development,[1] ego/self development,[2] cognitive development,[3] spiritual/faith development,[4] and at least eight others.[5] This article argues Palmer developed an integral perspective, and can be understood as an early leader of the integral age.[6]

The most complete way to examine Palmer's life is to use the Integral framework developed by philosopher Ken Wilber.[7] Known as Integral Theory, the framework includes first-, second-, and third- person perspectives combining many elements of human insight and knowledge.[8] It has been applied to dozens of disciplines from personal growth to politics, psychology to science, economics to subtle energies, and consciousness studies to ecology. This article applies Integral Theory to biography. Integral biography is a way to examine an individual's life while including the increasing levels of complexity, which develop through cultural, social, subjective, and behavioral domains. Such an approach is perfectly suited for a luminary like Palmer.

As the president of the first chiropractic school from 1906 to 1961, author of over 30 books, "developer" of chiropractic, and founder of the first radio station west of the Mississippi River, Palmer was instrumental in the early growth of what is today the third largest health profession. The chiropractic profession grew from 50 doctors of chiropractic in 1904 to over 70,000 today. The depth and breadth of Palmer's legacy is difficult to ascertain. He was an inspiration to thousands of followers, and sometime lightning rod for conflict and dissension. Except for chiropractors, who follow the direct professional lineage initiated the first chiropractor, and Palmer's father, Daniel David "D.D.," very few know of him.

Palmer struggled to break new ground and establish a legacy for chiropractic and the principles it rests upon; that there is an innate intelligence organizing the body, and it is superior to the educated intelligence (the conscious thinking mind), as it is the link to the universal intelligence in the cosmos and a source for guidance in life as well as health.[9] Chiropractic for Palmer was an injunction for man to be aligned with the flow of this inner intelligence and ideally with the infinite wisdom infusing all matter. This could be achieved through the injunction of the chiropractic adjustment.[10] In his push to advance this unique form of perennial wisdom, Palmer became author, teacher, businessman, traveler, and for many, carrier of a sacred torch.[11] Inspired by his early experiences, Palmer went on to live an extraordinary life, punctuated by peak states, crises, and fresh insights into the depths of what it is to be human.

An important aspect of integral biography is to acknowledge the influence social and cultural forces have in the shaping of the subject's life. There is little room in this article to describe the social and cultural history leading up to Palmer's insights and development. Some of this history has been written elsewhere.[12] An integral perspective on this historical and cultural legacy has also been undertaken.[13] Explicit links have been made to the origins of Palmer's ideas and worldview in a lineage stretching to antiquity and culminating in the metaphysical movements of nineteenth century America.[14] Palmer and his father attempted to provide an injunction linking the One and the many,[15] healing the fracture of the modern world between science, art, and spirituality.[16] Palmer's insights hardly stand alone yet in his particular style, worldview, and life circumstances; they are a contribution to the evolution of consciousness and the furthering of integral approaches to health, healing, and embodied enlightenment.

Social and cultural forces also influence the author and the reader. The author expresses the worldview conveyed through the text and the reader interprets the text through their own worldview. As to my own perspective, as the biographer, my influences are many. I am in a direct lineage from Palmer. The founder of the school in which I studied chiropractic was a student at Palmer's school while he lived. I am also a long-term student of human development, consciousness studies, and philosophy, which gives me a unique perspective on Palmer's role in the history of ideas. I have been studying Palmer's life and writings now for fourteen years. Thus I will aim for accuracy, honesty, and a check on any tendency to over-glorify or exaggerate Palmer's life and accomplishments. And as to you, the reader, I only ask that you suspend all preconceived notions you may have about chiropractic. This is an important point, as the social and cultural forces that have shaped modern-day chiropractic have also influenced common perceptions and misconceptions, which, if not checked at the outset could interfere with an objective look at Palmer's life as a unique human being.

Literature Review

This review of the literature describes the documents relating to integral biography and the few writings on Palmer's life. Some of the literature on

Integral Theory and the methodologies comprising it will be described throughout the article as reference material.

There is not much literature on integral biography. The closest peer-reviewed article to the topic is on integral leadership.[17] Thierry Pauchant has proposed an ambitious project to write 100 "leadographies" of integral leaders from Plato to Lincoln to Eleanor Roosevelt and Gandhi, using Integral Theory as a lens for each biography.[18] The goal would then be to compare the lives of each leader and tease out the common threads. It is a brilliant approach to examine many individuals through all domains of their development, subjectively, intersubjectively, objectively, and interobjectively. In this way, it proposes to test the veracity of Integral Theory in real lives played out through time, and how real people developed to become integral leaders. In order to scientifically determine the integral level of leaders requires specific criteria, methodology, research design, and research strategies.[19]

Pauchant offers three retrospective criteria to examine multiple lines of development and determine whether a leader was integral; the leader must have had a significant impact on a community or organization, there must be a general consensus amongst a diverse population that the leader was well respected, and the leader must have been viewed by others as "post-conventional," with a de-centered ego. A fourth objective criterion is to analyze the individual's life and development through the lens of Integral Theory. Retrospective analysis is suggested for two reasons; 1) it takes decades for the integral level to unfold for an individual and 2) research indicates about 1-2% of the population is at the integral level.[20] It is proposed the leader must meet the first three criteria in order to rule out individuals who were not integral leaders. Data sources to verify these criteria include obituaries, biographies, autobiographies, letters, interviews, and other documents on the individual's life. Pauchant writes, "Integral leaders are described by words and expressions such as "saint," "elevated soul," "spiritual," "enlightened," "kindred spirit," possessing a "sacred wisdom," being "spiritually virtuous," "divinely inspired," "selfless," etc.[21] Other indicators of the leader's integral nature include openness to new possibilities as opposed to rigid adherence to values, beliefs, and dogma.

Pauchant also proposes several methods to do such an integral biography. Various methodologies should include interpretive biography (to capture the subjective, personal, and behavioral aspects of the individual), institutional analysis (to study how the leader led an organization differently from typical leaders), and historical inquiry (to place the leader in a social and cultural context). A story or vignette along with a good quote and photograph may be sufficient to capture each stage of development within the context of the life story. And, unlike the classic biography focused on a hero or heroine, the leader should be placed in a life; the social and cultural forces shaping and being shaped by the individual are very important. Pauchant even goes so far as to suggest the biography should begin with an emphasis on objective actions and interactions with others and then focus on the personal and interpersonal more interior and cultural aspects.

An emphasis should be placed on the leader's growth and development, often marked by epiphanies and crucibles. Pauchant's emphasis on "crucibles of leadership" and epiphanies is even more important for a brief biographical study such as this one. Crucibles are defined as moments in the individual's life that act as a turning point, usually marked by crisis, forced reflection, loss, or mentors.[22] Epiphanies are new moments of insight, which sometimes accompany a new level of consciousness. Denzin writes epiphanies, "radically alter and shape the meanings persons give to themselves and their life projects. In epiphanies, personal character is manifested and made apparent."[23] Following Pauchant's lead, and due to limited space, Palmer's story will center on such moments.

Pauchant suggests that developmental survey instruments are not the best way to measure the level (also referred to by Wilber as *altitude*) of integral leaders, in part, from the reasons above and because such instruments focus on one line of development only, such as ego, or morals, or cognition.[24] This is supported by the recent work of Zachary Stein. Based on his empirical research and rooted in the ideas of Habermas, Stein, suggests developmental survey instruments, reconstruct a deeper intuitive knowledge all humans naturally have.[25] That is, humans intuitively know what altitude others are at. This intuition gets better with age and experience, knowledge of the developmental literature and in the case of this researcher (me), Palmer's own works. Therefore, intuition of altitude is a valuable addition to Pauchant's detailed approach because it supports Pauchant's third criteria, that the individual is viewed by others as post conventional.

Pauchant importantly notes there are three types of criticisms of individuals: critiques blatantly wrong, critiques from other levels of development, and critiques that are accurate.[26] In the writings about Palmer, we find all of these types of criticism.

The literature on B.J. Palmer is significant; his autobiographical writings are many. An entire discipline exists around chiropractic history, including a journal, an organization, and an annual academic conference. The conference is hosted by the Association for Chiropractic History, and is held in a different chiropractic school each year. Although there have been many popular articles, peer-reviewed articles, and book sections or chapters about B.J. Palmer,[27] there are only a few books about him; an explicit biography[28] and other "family" biographies and treatises.[29] Very little of the research to date takes a deep look at Palmer in accordance with the levels of consciousness he developed through.[30] This is one reason why an integral biography is vital as too much gets lost with cross-level criticism and a lack of depth.

The main difference between *integral biography* and Pauchant's "leadographies" is the focus of the study. The Integral framework can be applied to any person's life resulting in an integral biography. A leadography is about an integral leader. Since the life of Palmer fits so closely to the concept of the integral leader, Pauchant's roadmap is ideal for this article. The case can be made that Palmer was an integral leader in his later years as he matured into the integral level of consciousness, by that point however, it was probably too late to extend his impact beyond his most loyal followers. From age 68 until his death at age 79, he wrote sixteen books totaling 7,990 pages.[31] Palmer's nephew William Heath Quigley wrote how Palmer hoped the books would be his greatest legacy.[32]

Methods

We will begin by determining whether Palmer meets Pauchant's first three criteria. The article will then offer a discussion of Integral Theory (Pauchant's fourth criteria). The rest of the article will use Integral Theory to explore the person B.J. became, his insights and personal experiences, and the ingredients which may have helped him to get there. Rather than a 150 page "leadography" as suggested by Pauchant, this article will highlight five crucibles of Palmer's development, marking transitions between levels of consciousness, with an emphasis on his circumstance, epiphanies, and new worldviews.

Assessing Palmer's Level and Legacy

Pauchant's first three criteria are important to rule out whether Palmer was Integral or not. Did Palmer have a significant impact on a community or organization? Yes. Was he highly regarded by a diverse population? Yes. Was he considered to be post-formal with a de-centered ego? Based on the remembrances of Palmer by his former students and faculty (Appendix A), and an objective assessment of a sample of his writings by Susanne Cook-Greuter (Appendix B), both described below, I will conclude that Palmer meets the third criteria and thus all three criteria of integral leadership.

In 1990, there was a special tribute to Palmer in the magazine, *Today's Chiropractic*. Several of Palmer's former students and faculty were asked to reminisce about him. A summary of the quotes (see Appendix A) are as follows; being with B.J. refreshed one, his presence gave people fortitude that would last decades, his charisma and mostly his eyes were magnetic, he looked into your soul, his presence was hypnotic, he was powerful, he was "a rainmaker," he was gentle and filled with love, and his mission to heal a sick world was gigantic and compelling.[33] Finally, his biographer, Joe Maynard wrote,

> Many men and women experienced personal development after having come in contact with B.J. Palmer, because he had the innate ability to bring forth the innate creative substance that is buried deep in every individual, allowing this creativity to surface and be experienced in one's living.[34]

Palmer was viewed in positive light and as a powerful presence by many, which compelled people to dedicate their lives to his vision.

Another more objective assessment of Palmer's later writings was examined for this article by Susanne Cook-Greuter. Cook-Greuter is a leader in the field of adult development. She determines an individual's level of ego or self development based on linguistic analysis using a Sentence Completion Test (SCT).[35] I asked her to analyze a famous passage of B.J.'s, in which he describes one of his greatest epiphanies, and thereafter referred to himself as "We" rather than "I." The passage and this epiphany are discussed in more context below in the section on Palmer's later development. Excerpts of the passage with Cook-Greuter's assessment are included as Appendix B. Her retrospective analysis can be considered an intuition of altitude. In the analysis, Cook-Greuter points to the fact that Palmer's language is clearly at the level above integral, or 5/6 on her 6 part scale of human development, indicating a post-conventional perspective and de-centered although still bounded ego. Cook-Greuter wrote,

> Overall, Palmer's writing seems to come from an advanced personal perspective with occasional forays and intimations of transpersonal experience…The insistence on duality in the description of two selves in one would be scored at stage 5/6, the last stage of post conventional development in the personal rationally-mediated realm.[36]

Palmer's post conventional development will be described in more detail towards the end of the article after first describing his earlier transitions between stages and their accompanying crucibles and epiphanies.

The AQAL Framework

Analysis using Wilber's framework is Pauchant's fourth criteria to determine whether the leader was integral or not. Wilber writes, "One of the main difficulties in presenting the Integral approach is that you have to explain it before you can apply it."[37] Wilber's framework, also known as the AQAL model, includes five elements: quadrants, levels, lines, states, and types. In order for a biography to be considered integral, it needs to include at least quadrants and levels. The more elements of the framework are included, the more integral the biography will be. In the case of B.J. Palmer, it is important to include states, lines, quadrants, and levels. *Types* have more to do with his style of management, personality style, extrovert/introvert, or other measures of how he acted through all of his levels. Types are not essential for understanding the levels he may have developed to. *States* refers to states of consciousness such as epiphanies and altered states. This will be described when appropriate throughout the life story. The other elements, quadrants, levels, and lines will be defined and then incorporated into his life story.

Quadrants

The four *quadrants* are the most basic and irreducible perspectives you can take on any event in the universe. The quadrants are the map through which we can view each domain of Palmer's life. In the Upper-Left quadrant (UL), a person experiences their own interior and subjective experience ("I"). This is where we can view Palmer's levels, lines, types, and states of consciousness. In the Upper-Right quadrant (UR), we can discuss Palmer's actions, behaviors, and his bodily states such as his physical experience as a chiropractor for 60 years, or the changes in his brainwaves while in hypnotic or contemplative states ("It"). The Lower-Left quadrant (LL) is the domain of interpersonal resonance, shared meaning and culture ("We"). This is where we can discuss cultural influences on Palmer, and Palmer's ability or inability to connect with others, influential orations, his philosophical outreach efforts to establish an integral profession, as well as his cultural impact beyond chiropractic as an integral pioneer. The Lower-Right quadrant (LR) is the interobjective domain; social systems, ecology, or any domain where two or more individuals are gathered ("Its"). Here we can discuss Palmer's social circumstances, economic realities, the development of a school, a profession, and any other social interactions he may have had in his life.

Levels

Wilber developed the concept *altitude of development*,[38] to unite the many approaches to developmental research. The basic core of this approach is an acknowledgement that there are at least a dozen empirically valid methods to measure human development from infancy well into adulthood. Wilber color-coded these levels for the sake of simplicity (Table 1). Each color represents a general altitude of consciousness, which can act as a measure for all of the different lines of development. Pauchant emphasizes Wilber's concept of soft-stages, that is, individuals oscillate around a various stage with a "center of gravity" rather than ossifying at any one stage.[39] This is a helpful way through which to observe Palmer's development, especially in regards to unbalanced lines of development.

Lines

The self's many aspects develop through these broad levels or altitudes, in lines of development. Each line develops independently from the rest, but they are intricately connected. The two most notable are self and cognition. The self navigates and ties together all of the lines, while cognition or knowing usually leads development. There are unlimited ways to measure how many levels exist in each line and many researchers use seven or more levels. Unbalanced development is common, as some lines generally develop faster than others. We can observe uneven development throughout Palmer's life; for example, he had very well developed cognitive and spiritual lines although his interpersonal lines seemed less developed, as noted below in his relationships with his family and others in the profession.

We will examine four of Palmer's lines of development. These are self ("who am I?"), cognition ("what am I aware of?"), values ("what is significant to me?"), and spirituality/faith ("what is of ultimate concern?").[40] To gauge Palmer's development, we will examine his writings, his actions, and his legacy primarily along these four lines. While not discussing Palmer's aesthetic line in detail, it was certainly well developed, evidenced by his eclectic mansion, mode of dress, myriad collections, and extensive gardens.[41] And as noted, he had challenges in his interpersonal line.

Each new altitude is a wider embrace, an increase in complexity and perspective, such as the journey from egocentric to ethnocentric to worldcentric. The first six altitudes represent development from infancy to adulthood and the beginnings of a worldcentric worldview. The integral altitude is often referred to as post-conventional and post-formal. It is represented by Teal and Turquoise stages of consciousness. It is possible Palmer experienced levels beyond Turquoise, but there is no evidence that his center of gravity was there. Descriptions of Palmer's life at each altitude will only be an approximation. The complexity and empirical research behind each line within each altitude is not captured in such a brief description. (For a more detailed understanding, the reader is directed to the references in Table 1).

I hypothesize Palmer's development was driven by his cognitive line, and more specifically, his subtle-cognition. Cognition can be viewed along three streams: gross, subtle, and causal.[42] Each of these streams develops independently. Gross cognition ceases development after thought begins to reflect on itself. This type of self-reflection involves

Turquoise	High Vision-Logic (Cross-Paradigmatic) (Higher or Global Mind)	Intuitive (BO/Turquoise)	Construct-Aware (Ingegrated, Magician)	Universalizing-Commonwealth
Teal	Low Vision-Logic (Paradigmatic)	Systemic (AN/Yellow)	Autonomous (Strategist)	Universalizing-Commonwealth
Green	Pluralistic Mind (Meta-Systemic) (Planetary Mind)	Relativistic (FS/Green)	Individualistic(Individualist)	Paradoxical-Consolidative (Conjunctive)
Orange	Formal Operational (Rational Mind)	Multiplistic (ER/Orange)	Conscientious (Achiever) Self-Aware (Expert)	Individuative-Reflective
Amber	Concrete Operational (Rule/Role Mind)	Absolutistic (DZ/Blue)	Conformist (Diplomat)	Synthetic-Conventional
Red	Preoperational (Conceptual)	Egocentric (CP/Red)	Self-Protective	Mythic-Literal
Magenta	Preoperational (Symbolic)	Animistic (BO/Purlple)	Impulsive	Intuitive-Projective (Magical)
Infrared	Sensorimotor	Autistic (AN/Beige)	pre-social and symbiotic	Undifferentiated faith
	Cognition	Values	Self	Faith
	Piaget/Commons Richards/Aurobindo	Graves/Beck Cowan/Wade	Loevinger Cook-Greuter	Fowler

Table 1 Four lines in eight altitudes (Wilber, 2006; Brown, 2007)

subtle cognition as the individual no longer reflects on the gross physical world, but on the subtle world of thoughts, imagination, and concepts. Subtle cognition is evident in early childhood, and then reappears in a mature form in later development. Throughout development, it may be cultivated through techniques such as hypnosis and contemplation, and these can lead to the development of causal cognition.[43] Hypnosis and contemplation were two of Palmer's primary techniques of self-development, and they pushed his development forward throughout his life. Preliminary evidence of the leadographies shows all integral leaders have a regular practice of meditation or prayer.[44] Palmer did as well, and from an early age.

B.J. Palmer's Evolution

B.J. Palmer's development was marked by at least five identifiable crucibles. Warren Bennis and Robert Thomas define a crucible as "a transformative experience through which an individual comes to a new or an altered sense of identity."[45] Such crucibles can involve overcoming prejudice or insurmountable challenges, or being pushed on by a mentor. More specifically, Thomas names four types of crucibles; enforced reflection, mentoring relationships, immersion in a foreign land, and disruption/loss.[46] True leaders emerge from crucibles with what Bennis and Thomas call "adaptive capacity," the ability to creatively and almost magically emerge stronger than before. I suggest that each of Palmer's primary five crucibles were transitions from one soft-stage to the next, one altitude to a more embracing and adaptive one.

The rest of the article will examine each crucible in terms of four quadrants, four lines, important epiphanies, and altitude. The five transitions/crucibles based on my intuition of Palmer's altitudes are as follows; his move from a Red altitude to Amber (between 1895-1903), his move from Amber altitude to Amber/Orange (between 1907-1924), his move from Orange/Amber to Orange/Green (between 1924-1949), his move from Green to Teal (1948-1953), his move from Teal to Turquoise (1953-1957). Due to the available space, only a bare outline will be provided for Palmer's first four crucibles. Emphasis is placed on his final levels of development, in order to determine just how integrally developed he may have been.

The First Crucible:
Palmer's Transition from Red to Amber

In Palmer's writings about his childhood and teenage years, he recounts a difficult childhood with time living on the streets.[47] This was his Red altitude, centered on the egocentric self. Two of his biographers described the harshness of a demanding father,[48] and an even more demanding step-mother.[49] B.J. was expelled from high school in 1895 (for releasing the white mice in order to get the girls to jump on their chairs), the year attributed to the first chiropractic adjustment by his father.[50]

In order to "straighten" his son out, D.D. Palmer, a former magnetic healer and an avid Spiritualist, sent B.J. on tour with Professor Flint, a vaudeville hypnotist, for two seasons in 1899 (LR). It was with Flint, that B.J. learned to cultivate his inner depths (UL) and master the art of meditative hypnotic trance.[51] It is also at this time, between the ages of 17-19, when Palmer claims to have "found himself" in relation to the principle of innate intelligence and universal intelligence.[52] After this first epiphany, he soon became a doctor of chiropractic (UR) and after a series of legal cases against him and his father; B.J. was forced to take over the leadership of the school in 1902, and eventually the profession (LR/LL).

I suggest Palmer used this moment as a leadership crucible.[53] He utilized the mentorships of Flint and his father. He learned to access inner states (Thomas' enforced introspection) from the deep hypnotic trances taught to him by Flint.[54] Palmer also developed internal energies and dedicated his life to an inner contemplation of the relationship between matter, life, and Spirit.[55] His contemplation, given to him by his father, of the link between innate intelligence and universal intelligence and chiropractic's role in that linkage became a daily meditation, a spiritual practice, and a subtle practice.[56] This meditation was presumably made experiential through his hypnotic states, his reception of chiropractic adjustments, and his mastery as a practitioner and teacher of chiropractic. With these new inner resources, he became a leader.

Palmer's line of subtle-cognition was the driver for his personal evolution for the rest of his days. Lerner suggested that Palmer used his new ability of "self-hypnosis" to take on new persona, such as professional leader for the next fifty years.[57] The line of subtle cognition takes interior states as its referents.[58] Subtle cognition is thought acting on thought as well as creativity, imagination, reverie, illumination, meditative, hypnogogic and hypnotic states. Since cognition generally leads the way for the other lines of development, B.J.'s subtle cognition led the development of his values, faith, and self.

The Second Crucible:
Palmer's Transition from Amber to Orange

At the Amber altitude, individuals seek to fit into society and develop a rigid value system of right and wrong. They exhibit ethnocentric, conventional, and conformist attributes. The limbic system, which governs emotions, dominates the self at this level of consciousness. It is also characterized by logical inconsistencies, where science is valued only when it supports "the truth".[59] Here, the individual is most interested in the "in-group," such as friends and family. Those who are outside of the group are largely rejected.[60]

From 1902, when he received his chiropractic degree (UR), until 1907, when he helped to win a landmark case for chiropractic's legal scope, Palmer's self and values were firmly rooted in the Amber altitude (UL). The social (LR) and cultural (LL) climate helped to shape Palmer's development.[61] He became conventional in the outward aspects of society such as getting married, starting a family (his son David was born in 1906), purchasing a 22-room mansion (1912), running an institution, and guiding the initial years of a profession.[62]

Palmer's uneven development was inevitable (UL). At the heart of his conforming and conventional self and values, was his post-conventional profession with its radical philosophy, i.e., the chiropractic adjustment unlocked the hidden potentials of health, sanity, and enlightenment. The philosophy continued to push his development. And yet, he codified his philosophic approach to defend his father's legacy and his life's vision, along with his livelihood. He fought to develop an alternative health profession in the face of incredible pressures from the newly organized medical profession.[63]

This crucible came to a head while his father still lived, causing great interpersonal stress between father and son (and resulting in false charges of patricide after D.D.'s death in 1913).[64] B.J. forced the legal issues in the courts by instigating the landmark Morikubo vs. Wisconsin case.[65]

This was the first legal case to establish chiropractic as a separate and distinct profession. It catapulted B.J. to a new level of leadership, with the start of his organization, the Universal Chiropractors' Association. With mentors of Tom Morris (his legal counsel) and Elbert Hubbard, the eclectic founder of Roycrofters, B.J. evolved in his consciousness and took many new actions. He began to dress and write like Hubbard with his long hair, a flowing tie, and the shortening of words such as "thot" for "thought".[66] Inspired by Hubbard, B.J. also began to cover the campus with hundreds of epigrams.[67] Palmer started publishing books, fighting legal battles (3,300 by the 1920s), and expanding the school enrollment dramatically.[68] Palmer's quick rise to the leadership of the new profession would soon meet great obstacles.

The Third Crucible:
Palmer's transition from Amber/Orange to Orange/Green

The self at the Orange altitude is focused on individualism, objective criteria for truth, and rationality. From the time he became the president of the Palmer School of Chiropractic in 1906 to the opening of his research clinic in 1935, B.J. wrote fourteen books, started a printing press, owned two radio stations, taught classes around the country and the world, traveled the world three times, and expanded chiropractic into a global profession. Science, individualism, and the pursuit of the truth of chiropractic were his early guides.

Entrepreneurship and advertising were two of B.J.'s gifts. His attitude of success permeated all he did and was strewn across the campus in the form of epigrams such as, "He that bloweth not his own horn, for him shall no horn be blown," and, "Early to bed, early to rise, Work like hell—and advertise."[69] As a radio pioneer, he owned two stations, broadcasting chiropractic programs as well as others programming nation-wide. In 1942 he published, *Radio Salesmanship: how its potential sales percentage can be increased.* Palmer was even considered a motivational inspiration by Napoleon Hill in 1920, and gave Ronald Reagan his first job as an announcer.[70]

Palmer's lines continue to unevenly diverge from this point. His sense of self and values are deeply entwined at Amber, with proving chiropractic and maintaining his leadership very important. His nephew, W.H. Quigley wrote, "He often said, 'If you're not for me, then you're against me.' This facet of his personality can be seen to play a major role in his life and destiny."[71] His cognition centers on Orange as a dominant "center of gravity" from around 1910 with his introduction of x-rays into the profession until the 1950s. This drive, coupled with lingering gravity in Amber, often impacted his relationships and created the type of crucible Thomas would define as loss/disruption.[72]

Palmer's attempts to embrace science met with great resistance from his followers. In 1924, he introduced the Neurocalometer, an early thermography device, in hopes of combining objective readings into chiropractic analysis. His insistence all chiropractors should use the device and lease them from his school, led to his core faculty starting their own school and his decline as leader of the growing profession.[73] Maynard wrote the stress was so overwhelming from the extensive criticism, Palmer had a breakdown, spent a short time in Pass Christian, a sanitarium in Mississippi, and eventually healed himself by collecting glacial rocks and boulders by the ton from the banks of the Mississippi River, which were used to build a gigantic garden on the campus during 1923 and 1924. One of his students, Ester Mork wrote, "I often heard B.J. say that building the Little Bit O' Heaven saved his sanity."[74] The construction of this garden could be viewed as a two-year long meditation for Palmer, a deepening of his subtle cognition, his spiritual line, as well as his self and values.

The Fourth Crucible:
Palmer's Transition to Green

The Green altitude is marked by contextual thinking, sensitivity, equalitarianism, as well as an ability to reflect on the self in more complex ways. This crucible happened for Palmer over several years as a result of the crises he faced, his travels, and his research.

At the height of these crises, B.J. traveled the world three times with his wife Mabel and his son Dave. Travel to foreign lands is a potential crucible.[75] This pivotal and transitional time allowed Palmer to grow in his sensitivity, compassion, vision, inspiration and spirituality.[76] He also introduced the upper-cervical chiropractic technique in 1933, and opened the B.J. Palmer Research Clinic in 1935. Combined, these events were to profoundly transform Palmer. Since he was focused on "researching the unknown man" for 14 years,[77] it is difficult to ascertain when Palmer may have transitioned to a mature Green center of gravity. We already know that he was contemplating pluralistic, holistic, and post-conventional philosophies and transpersonal awareness for most of his life. His father was probably one of the early Green pioneers.[78] There is however a vein of his voluminous writings in his final years that points to a pluralistic core. We can conjecture it developed during this crucible time of travel and research. He declared to the profession based on his empirical research he had developed the greatest technique the profession had yet known, the hole in one (HIO).

Through his writings in the 1950s, we can infer a profound transformation in values, spirituality, cognition, and perhaps his very self structure. His view of religion and medicine evolved to dismiss miracles, disparage hypocritical doctors, and embrace innate intelligence in a deeper way. For example, for Palmer, the idea of a virgin birth was an insult to the innate of Mary![79] In the same vein, he poked fun at doctors who pretended to believe in God and then tried to alter the body through drugs and surgery. A type of sacrilege to innate! He also began to write in terms of the relationship between the innate within and genius. Palmer shows a development in his spirituality and subtle cognition. He begins to interpret all truth as one and eventually all people as reflections of this oneness. The innate intelligence in each body is the same working principle in all. B.J. believed he had found the missing link between spirit and matter, for which humans had always searched. And this is where he transitioned from a rationalistic Orange altitude to Green and beyond to Integral.

The Fifth Crucible:
B.J.'s transition to Integral Consciousness

Cognition at the Teal altitude has more to do with the creation of new paradigms.[80] The self at Teal links practice with theory while understanding the interconnected systems and contexts involved and emphasizes the value of higher levels of development.[81] The body/mind is understood as a system and a person begins to reflect on the evolutionary unfolding of development itself. Intuition aids rational thought.[82] Values at Teal are focused on being.[83]

The premise of Palmer's new chiropractic technique, the upper cervical specific or HIO, was extremely holistic and based on two implied hierarchies. It was holistic because at its core was the principle that the innate intelligence does the adjustment, impacting the entire body, mind, and spirit, and the chiropractor only introduces a specific force in the right direction at the correct time. It was hierarchical because it categorized a major and minor subluxation (a misaligned vertebra, putting pressure on a nerve, and interfering with the flow of mental impulse from the innate intelligence) as well as compensatory distortions in other areas of the spine (and for society and culture, because the unsubluxated individual could then impact the world in more profound ways due to more ready access to Innate). The major and minor were always the top two vertebrae in the neck, C1 and C2. It was also hierarchic because it was based on the idea the central nervous system was the master controlling system of the body, controls, which originated at the brain, were dictated by the innate intelligence, and ultimately by the universal intelligence. Palmer created the B.J. Palmer Research Clinic to study this phenomenon.

This HIO technique and the research clinic came at the height of Palmer's Orange altitude, and both became vehicles for his transition through the Green altitude and into second-tier in regards to his cognition, self, values, and spirituality. Of the years of Palmer's research into these phenomena, Augustus Dye, who wrote, *The Evolution of*

Chiropractic, with B.J.'s assistance, noted how B.J. mellowed in his animosities towards his chiropractic enemies and his sensitivity increased, as he immersed himself in his research.[84]

Palmer's research in the clinic led him to study the subtle energies of the body.[85] He began to view the human organism as an energetic and spiritual being. He wrote, "It is true we are spiritual, using the body as an instrument."[86] Reports from diverse spiritual traditions suggest the contemplation of subtle energies accelerates one's development, especially along the spiritual and subtle cognitive lines.[87] Palmer developed verifiable proof to match his life of subtle contemplation.

Palmer understood the differences of developmental levels, which is a hallmark of Teal cognition. He viewed the conflicts between science and religion to be solvable by using rationality to embrace the intelligence immanent in matter and life.[88] He expected others to develop as he did, through a satori-like burst of subtle cognition. He did look back to his own development but credited his evolution to "that something" in the soul which opened him to circumstance, intuition, inner knowing and what we might call serendipity/synchronicity.[89]

The final crucible and second major epiphany for Palmer came around the time of his wife Mabel's death, just as he was completing his 14 years of research. Their relationship had been strained for years (with his son as well). This is another indication of Palmer's uneven development and may be a source of his growth into the next stage of development. Mabel bought a house in Tucson, Arizona, in the late 1930s. Except for visits back home, she stayed in Arizona until her death in 1949. In her will, Mabel left B.J.'s mansion and all of her stock in the school and the radio stations (which were in her name for legal reasons from years before), to her granddaughters. His nephew wrote, "It left him with a bitterness he was unable to exorcise."[90] After Mabel's death, Palmer wrote 16 books in 11 years. It is in these books that his higher development can be assessed.

Palmer's Turquoise Epiphany: I becomes We

Turquoise altitude represents cognition that crosses paradigms by creating new fields. Sri Aurobindo coined the term *Higher Mind* for this level; the spiritual inspiration for mind, especially in regards to big truth.[92] The self at this level is in conflict between a need to de-center the ego and to merge the self-consciousness with a larger and wider self-sense. The ego may be viewed as a great threat to future growth and the individual has great inner-tension.[93] It is this level that Cook-Greuter suggests Palmer wrote from in his final book (Appendix B).

In 1949, Palmer publicly announced the use of "We" and denounced the use of "I." All of his works from 1949-1953 have a disclaimer to the use of the term "We." In the preface to most of these books, he referred to the pronoun "I" as "disgusting," "egotistical," and "selfish." In regards to the pronoun "We," he acknowledged that it represented an inclusion of the innate, the educated mind, as well as all people working towards this new truth. Of this statement above, Cook-Greuter wrote:

Stage 5/6 is quintessentially about the person who has discovered the shenanigans of the ego, but has not yet permanently transcended the critical, constantly measuring stance towards reality. S/he is in a constant struggle to achieve transegoic states, but they have not developed into a stage or position from which one can systematically and consistently write. Thus, the vacillating voice, sometimes personal, other times transpersonal.[94]

In 1953, upon re-writing his 900 pages of notes and photos from his 1933 trip to the Buddhist temples of Cambodia, Palmer changed every pronoun of the manuscript from "I" to "We."[95] In terms of the quadrants, he spoke from the UL and UR as one voice, invoking the LL "We" and thereby challenging the LR, the societal, linguistic, and social standards. I suggest this very process of re-writing was a form of deepening his new insight and furthering his own development. In each of the sixteen books from 1949-1961, the pronoun used was "We."

In his 1961 book, *The Glory of Going On*, published posthumously, he tells the story of his enlightenment to this new way of speaking. He writes that he stopped "involving" and started "evolving" as few have or will. I asked Susanne Cook-Greuter to examine the language used in that chapter to determine whether Palmer's linguistic structures matched language that an individual uses at second or third tier in self development. Cook-Greuter concluded that Palmer was still stuck in a dualistic relationship (at least in this brief passage) and that he had some very clear transcendent and even nondual insights or states but his self or ego seemed to be at stages 5/6, Turquoise, or what she calls Construct-Aware (at the end of second tier). Cook-Greuter acknowledged that a context of his life would help, and it would have been best to have him take her developmental survey when he was still living![96] From this and the other evidence thus far, I suggest Palmer's self structure evolved driven by his subtle-cognition, his spirituality, and his values.

Spirituality at Teal and Turquoise is called Universalist by Fowler; it is rare.[97] Individuals at this level have a felt sense of a universal connection that they actualize in their life. They are usually "contagious," in the way they inspire movements, become martyrs, people like Martin Luther King Jr., Gandhi, and Mother Theresa.[98] I am not suggesting that Palmer developed fully in every line. And as to his spirituality, we would be hard pressed to compare him to Gandhi or Mother Theresa, but we can certainly view his impact on his followers and the world as the mark of a very advanced soul.

"Thot Flashes" in Turquoise

Palmer embraced a very deep intuitive voice that guided him in daily actions as well as in business.[99] He even carried a pad and pen with him at all times to write inspirations, especially at night by his bedside. He referred to these as "thot flashes" from universal to innate to educated. Wade describes this type of transformation as the Authentic level of the self, when mind and body are becoming one. This happens around the Turquoise altitude. Wade wrote, there is "a frank acknowledgement of the intuitive voice. . . accompanied by a cognitive sophistication far in advance of the 'gut' voice."[100] Palmer discussed his ability to listen to that "wee sma' voice."

The analysis of an integral leader should include any different ways the leader acted in business.[101] Palmer began to run his business on the advice flashed to him from Innate.[102] According to Aurobindo, with the Intuitive Mind (Turquoise), intuition "flashes" like lightning to the thoughts.[103] It acts as a transitional stage between mental and higher truth. Palmer wrote, "WHEN Innate thot-flashes came they MUST BE accepted for full face value and acted upon AT ONCE."[104] Palmer's board of directors eventually learned to listen to his "thot flashes" as well. It turned out extremely well on one occasion when innate told him to pay back NBC for the options they had purchased in his radio station. He had no obligation to do so. The president of NBC was so impressed that he invited Palmer to lunch whenever he visited New York.[105]

Transcendent and Psychic

At the Transcendent Stage (just above Turquoise, what Wilber calls Indigo altitude) it is common for individuals to develop paranormal abilities but not to make a big deal of them. These abilities are hinted at in some of the quotes in Appendix A. Marcus Bach was a religious scholar who led the services at Palmer's funeral and wrote *The Chiropractic Story*.[106] In the book, he describes his first meeting with B.J. in the 1940s. After describing the incredible oration B.J. gave to an annual homecoming audience of about 2,000 cheering chiropractors, Bach describes the meeting. He wrote, "Now that I had this nearness to him what were my impressions? His personality? Electric. His presence? Contagious. His influence? Provocative. His manner? Supernal." This is clearly a description meeting Pauchant's third criteria,[107] but there was more. Bach goes on to describe how Palmer was able to read his mind; they even discussed it openly. Bach continued, "Disturbed and thrilled by the apparent way in which this plural-personality called B.J. read my mind, I realized as never before that thoughts *are* things, lines of communication defying words, transmitted, as B.J. had correctly said, 'from spirit to spirit.'" As Bach reflected on B.J.'s ability to read his thoughts he continued, "What kind of an extra-sensory man was this?"[108] Finally, Bach concluded, "He was a receiving and sending station, turned on, tuned in, seeing with an inner eye, listening with an inner ear, speaking with an inner voice."[109] According to Bach, B.J. overflowed into so many fields from radio, to organ music, to art, to collecting, as a reflection of his passion for chiropractic, so that he was not consumed by the passion of his own inner fire. We might simply call this being integral, where one form can no longer hold you.

From Nature Mysticism to Deity Mysticism

Palmer began to view religion as the striving of man to commune with the infinite. His lifetime contemplative practice focusing on innate intelligence was a form of nature mysticism, a way to use nature itself as an object through which to experience spiritual depths. In his final years, there is ample evidence that Palmer's mysticism also evolved to a more subtle deity mysticism, where God becomes the object of meditation rather than nature.[110] This is similar to the drivers of his cognition from his early days, where his subtle cognition became a source of personal evolution. Now in his seventies, he came full circle and his spirituality became fully immersed in the subtle aspects of reality itself.

From 1949-1955, Palmer wrote about the relationship between the individual and the infinite. For example, "Innate Intelligence is the Great I am that I am. Innate is the internal source of all and everything."[111] His writing was still focused more on nature and innate, yet striving towards something deeper. Then his writing changed, and from 1957-1961, these types of writings are geared more towards awakening to the inner God.

To Palmer, God was the universal source of intelligence, which was the archetypal ground of all nature, a universal and individualized law. God as the infinite communicated to the finite through the innate intelligence.

Palmer's experience of deity mysticism was an evolution of years of nature mysticism and the culmination of a life dedicated to subtle cognition, spiritual growth, and a dedication to creating a better world. Palmer's deity mysticism is best depicted in his final writings about chiropractic and shows a dramatic evolution of his thinking about the traditional tenets of chiropractic theory. Chiropractic became a practical means to answer the questions of all religions while healing people in the meantime. To Palmer, chiropractic was a transformative practice and philosophy destined to change the world's focus on healing, life-force, and God as within. He even considered the chiropractor to be "an apostle to the living god" that manifests through the tissues of the body, spine, and nervous system.[112]

At Peace

B.J. Palmer died on May 27, 1961. Over 3,000 people attended his funeral in the old Masonic temple in Davenport.[113] A life of genuine search for the ultimate answers was completed. At his funeral, his son David confided with his biographer, Joe Maynard, "He's at peace now, Joe, the struggle is all over."[114]

Appendix A

Quotes about Palmer from some former students and faculty from 1990 issue of *Today's Chiropractic.*

"An hour or so with B.J. was more refreshing and meaningful than a week with anyone else in chiropractic."

"The strength that B.J. provided gave me the will to believe, and for more than 50 years I have not found that will to be wanting."

—L.E. Allen[1]

"B.J.'s presence was almost hypnotic to me. As a young lad, I would lock my eyes onto him and just stand there and stare. Such a personage was B.J! Such a presence of being he had!"

"The power of the man was omnipresent -- in his carriage, his charisma, his prestige and his presence of being."

"Today, I understand him, but it took me 50 years to do so."

—Fred Barge[2]

"Amy would say, 'B.J. knew he was making history. He was a rainmaker.'"

—E.L. Crowder[3]

"B.J. knew you by your Innate. He was a gentle man so full of love that no obstacle was too great to overcome to get the "Big Idea" of chiropractic to our sick world."

On her husband and 4 kids who were all chiropractors,

"Truly, we have been blessed and enriched by knowing B.J. Palmer, a man who reached out to our Innates to entwine our lives and help us complete the mission we were sent here to do."

—Helen Killeen Peet (1951 graduate)[4]

"When he began to speak, there was no warmup or pussyfooting around; it was as if he were Moses himself. His voice had a sharp, crisp Midwestern tone and was very authoritative. And he spoke as if he were THE ONE in authority, as if he had been given the torch and the message straight from the source."

—Sid Williams[6]

Appendix B

Email from Susanne Cook-Greuter to Simon Senzon, analyzing excerpts from B.J. Palmer's Glory of Going On (1961). Printed with permission.[1]

Dear Simon,

I had a look at the text samples of Palmer you sent and had the following response:

Overall, Palmer's writing seems to come from an advanced personal perspective with occasional forays and intimations of transpersonal experience.

This book, so far as the author is concerned, writes from the duality of personalities-the inseparable, indivisible, Siamese-twin personalities living in the one structure-the Innate and Educated individualities.

The insistence on duality in the description of two selves in one (even though one is a super ordinate sense of historical connection) would be scored at stage 5/6, the last stage of post conventional development in the personal rationally-mediated realm. Palmer is much beholden to the "scientific" camp, understandably, but there is a way of writing that does not use as much judgmental language or absolute pronouncements (always, never) in assessing previous approaches and other people's current ones.

It eliminates that disgusting and egotistical selfish pronoun "I" which constantly intrudes itself.

Stage 5/6 is quintessentially about the person who has discovered the shenanigans of the ego, but has not yet permanently transcended the critical, constantly measuring stance towards reality. S/he is in a constant struggle to achieve transegoic states, but they have not developed into a stage or position from which one can systematically and consistently write. Thus, the vacillating voice, sometimes personal, other times transpersonal.

It is one of the biggest dilemmas in our field that it is exquisitely challenging to write in a transpersonal voice. I don't know how to do it except occasionally when in a reverie or other non-rational state. But I am not even sure of that. Wilber does manage to write in "One Taste" a clearly non-egoic voice.

It is not generally known I possess MANY degrees from MANY universities throut the world. What kind of universities are these? Where are they located? They are all universities of Hard Knocks. Surprisingly all are located in ONE city, in ONE building, in ONE room, in Davenport, at the P.S.C. in its Osteological Laboratory. *5/6,1*

I gazed, bewildered, at the many ramifications OF THOSE universities; looked about stupefied not knowing what to think, where to begin, what to do. It is not generally known I also hold degrees of caveologist, volcanologist, materialist, spiritualist, archeologist, humanitarian, historian, osteologist, and anthropologist.

These silent reminders of long past existences proved INNATE was an – architect, plumber, draughtsman, welder, engineer, fireman, builder, pump-maker, obstetrician, beautician, archeologist, artist, carpenter, erector of power stations, brick-layer, bridge-builder, layer of underground water systems in all its city streets, alleys, and homes, electrician, camera equipped with automatic adjustable lens, endless tape recorder, musical composer, ranging from grand opera to boogie woogie, color motion picture, thermostat, regulating heating and cooling air conditioner mechanic, sculptor, and then producing and reproducing patterns and products many times-a-one-unit, self-contained unit being. (need to be comprehensive, 5/6, 1)

The paragraphs above have a distinctly 5/6 flavor, a need to be as comprehensive as possible, at the same time, there is a kind of creativity visible that hints at postpostconventional possibilities. There is no expressed awareness that the One Room could be a different one for every person, which would be a more transegoic statement. The text is very focused on his own experience and there is little attempt to look around. On the other hand, the very form of total immersion into the object and his absorption in looking Palmer used, is an aspect of flow states. It is not altogether that rare in descriptions of scientific discovery and creativity.

I also get it that Palmer was an outsider and had to "fight" incredible odds in terms of being taken seriously for his discoveries.

In this ONE room is the GREATEST universities in the world, where time is and is not, was and was not surrounded by the essence of vast numbers of human realities.

Here we have the conjoining of polar opposites where A is both A and not-A; or neither A and not-A. To realize this and apply it in one's living is a transpersonal capacity. Understanding the post Aristotelian axiom logically is possible at stage 5/6.

I approached the multiple doors of this ONE room with hesitation and fear. Dared I open locked doors and boldly walk in? <u>Had I a right to disturb those long-lost sleeps of thousands of tragic souls who were hastened to untimely graves?</u> Had I courage sufficient to dig into their graves, open their coffins, and ask them to tell ME how they died? 5/6,2

The evaluative casting of these souls as tragic only with no alternative possibilities again would be more typical of a not yet self-transcendent type of writing.

Because therein IS THE KEY that opens and/or closes ALL doors to ALL knowledge of ALL living unrivaled human activities.

If it said therein is "one of many keys" or "my personal key although there are surely others in the universe," this would be more transegoic.

It was here I dreamed about and had abundance of proof of an incompetent, inefficient world of sick people, to find if possible an escape to conquer, to rehabilitate, to rejuvenate and rebuild, that those who live might be better, brighter, and happier. (I not included)

Again the all negative casting makes me wonder and the "I not included" raises questions of hubris for me. Why would one want to except oneself? The problem with short excerpts is that they can be quite misleading without the content of the rest of the writing. Moreover, this is my first encounter with this man's writing and personal and historical context would further help to interpret the observations I can make with the little I have.

The misfortunes of each were different-no two alike- as they must have performed their daily chores. The MATTER changed from one family to another, one century to another, but eh spirit, ego, soul, personality of the Innate that once lived in each of those homes all spoke ONE universal language, regardless of differences of race, color, nationality, geography, or of the century.

The above paragraph would be scored ego-transcendent as it is all-embracing.

These communing personalities of coming-to-life living people were and are an open book, reciting woes, worries, and how they struggled in conflicts within themselves to exist, handicapped with multitudes of insurmountable odds. Positive entirely left out.

Again, I miss a more equitable, less evaluative stance. The Innate in some of the bones must also have spoken of healing, joys, etc. and neutral traces not just negative ones. The attention to one side of a polar opposite and valuing over the other "health over illness" is distinctly ego-bound.

IN THAT ONE ROOM, I listened to, saw, and understood the brilliance of Innate Intelligence as it toiled, struggled, day after day, week after week, year after year, reshaping, mending, stitching together broken parts, replacing dead tissues with live ones, working consistently side by side with sicknesses and healths, as it toiled to keep those homes intact against the ravages of violence, disasters, wars, storms; and then, when it left that living home, it left behind an indelible record of how "wonderfully and fearfully" it performed its silent miracles to us uneducated people.

Let me finish with this last paragraph which shows the beginning integration of opposites. Palmer here briefly recognizes that sicknesses and healths are side by side. We do not have evidence however that he sees them as two sides of the same coin, that he is considering the possibility of an underlying reality that is undivided, non-dual. Overall diagnosis from these few paragraphs. A man at the cusp of personal development with intimations of transegoic perceptions and rare excursions into a less evaluative (evenly accepting), less self-conscious, transegoic voice.

The last paragraph also resonated with me as the task you posed felt wonderfully and fearfully challenging. It certainly made me step out of my zone of comfort! So take it all with a sea of salt. I would appreciate a response in terms of what makes sense and what doesn't. Thanks for the challenge!

Susanne

P.S. I do feel on surer ground scientifically if I have an actual Sentence Completion Test to work from.

Endnotes

Preface

1. Spizzerinctum is a term Palmer coined. It means, "Chiropractic enthusiasm."

Introduction

1. Webb, H. (1952). Evolution of the epigram. *Peabody Journal of Education*, 30(1), 22-26.

2. Nixon, P. (1927). *Martial and the modern epigram*. New York: Longmans, Green and Co., p. 29.

3. Wright, M. (1870). *The moral aphorisms and terseological teachings of Confucius: The sapient Chinese philosopher*. Battle Creek, Michigan: Published for the Author. For a reproduction of the 100 aphorisms see Senzon, S.A. (2007). *Chiropractic foundations: D.D. Palmer's traveling library*.

4. Gromola, T. (1985). Broadsides, epigrams, and testimonials: The evolution of chiropractic advertising. *Chiropractic History*, 4(1), 41-45.
    Wiese, G. (2003). With head, heart, and hands: Elbert Hubbard's impact on B.J. Palmer *Chiropractic History*, 23(2), 27-35.

5. Palmer, B.J. (1950). *Up from below the bottom*. Davenport, IA: PSC, p. 490.

6. Palmer, B.J. (1988). *As a man thinketh*. Davenport, Iowa:Delta Sigma Chi.
    Wiese, G. (2003). With head, heart, and hands.

7. Hubbard, E. (1911). *A thousand & one epigrams*: *Selected from the writings of Elbert Hubbard*. East Aurora: Roycrofters.

8. Palmer, B.J. (1988). *As a man thinketh*.

9. Stechschulte, P. (2008). The writing on the wall new epigrams for Life University. *Today's Chiropractic Lifestyle*, Feb/Mar, 62-64.
    Palmer College website: B.J. Palmer's epigrams.
    Retrieved Nov 22, 2009 from: http://www.palmer.edu/history2.aspx?id=1142.

10. Special thanks to Glenda Weise for assisting in gathering these facts from the Palmer Library stacks.
    (Palmer was made honorary president of Delta Sigma Chi in 1913)

11. Palmer, B.J. (1988). *As a man thinketh*, p. 112.

12.   Hender, H. (1949). Prologue/preface. In Palmer, B.J. *The Bigness of fellow within*. Davenport, IA: Palmer College, p. xxiv.

13.   Palmer, B. J. (1950). *Up from below the bottom*. Palmer College, Davenport, IA. p. 443. Palmer, B.J. (1947). 6th ed. *Radio salesmanship*. Davenport, IA: PSC Press. Gromola, T. 1985. Broadsides, epigrams, and testimonials. Weise, G. 2003. With head, heart, and hands.

14.   Wardwell, W. (1992). *Chiropractic: History and evolution of a new profession*. St. Louis: Mosby.

15.   Gromoloa, T. Broadsides, epigrams, and testimonials, p.43-44.

16.   Martin, S. 1993. Chiropractic and the social context of medical technology, 1895-1925 *Technology and Culture*, 34(4): 808-834.
Wardwell, W. (1992). *Chiropractic: History and evolution of a new profession*. Villanueva-Russell, Y. (2008). An ideal-typical development of chiropractic, 1895-1961: Pursuing professional ends through entrepreneurial means. *Social Theory & Health*, 6: 250-272.

17.   Palmer, B.J. (1952). *Answers*. Davenport, IA: Palmer College, p. 426.

18.   Gelardi, T. (1999). *Inspirations*. Spartanburg, SC: Sherman College of Straight Chiropractic. Strauss, J. (1997). *Practice building for straight chiropractors*. Levitown, PA: FACE. Stechschulte, P. (2008). The writing on the wall. Palmer College (n.d.). B.J. Palmer's epigrams.

19.   Stout, R., Burns, S., Hall, VR, Patore, M. (Eds.). (1991). *Familiar chiropractic quotations: An index to sources of quotations relevant to chiropractic*. Davenport, Iowa: Palmer College of Chiropractic.

20.   Senzon, SA. (2004). *The spiritual writings of B.J. Palmer*.

21.   Senzon, SA. (submitted). B.J. Palmer: An integral biography. *Journal of Integral Theory and Practice*.

22.   Palmer, B.J. (1951). *History Repeats*. Hammond, Indiana: Conkey Co.,p. 239.
(Caps by BJ).

Chapter 1

1.   Palmer, B.J. (1949). *The bigness of fellow within*, p. 55.

2.   Palmer, B.J. (1957). *Evolution or revolution*. Davenport, IA: PSC, p.18.

Chapter 2

1.   Palmer, B.J. (1950). *Fight to climb*. Davenport, IA: PSC, p. 87.

Chapter 3

1.   Palmer, B.J. (1952). *Answers*, p. 73.

2.   Palmer, B.J. (1961). *The glory of going on.* Davenport, IA: PSC, p. 252.

3.   Palmer, B.J. (1952). *Answers*, pp. 70-1.

4.   Palmer, B.J. (1958). *Palmer's law of life.* Davenport, IA: PSC, p. 18.

Chapter 4

1.   Palmer, B.J. (1950). *Fight to climb*, p. 37.

2.   Palmer, B.J. (1961). *The glory of going on*, p. 62.

Chapter 5

1.   Palmer, B.J. (1957). *Evolution or revolution*, p. 91.

2.   Palmer, B.J. (1958). *Palmer's law of life*, p. 33.

Chapter 6

1.   The Greenbooks on CD-ROM, compiled by Rob Sinnott.

2.   Palmer, B.J. (1950). *Up from below the bottom.* Davenport, IA: PSC, p. 441.

3.   Ibid, p. 557.

4.   Ibid, p. 558.

5.   Ibid, p. 564.

Chapter 7

1.   Palmer, B.J. (1950). *Up from below the bottom*, p. 510.

Chapter 8

1.   Palmer, B.J. (1951). History Repeats, p. 747.

2.   Palmer, B.J. (1949). *The bigness of fellow within*, p. 54.

Chapter 9

1.   Palmer, B.J. (1950). *Up from below the bottom*, p. 841.

2.   Palmer, B.J. (1952). *Answers*, p. 294.

3.   To view photos of Flint and Marina similar to images described by B.J. please

goto The Wilgus Collection: http://brightbytes.com/collection/flints.html

4.   Palmer, B.J. (1950). *Fight to climb*, p. 92.

Chapter 10

1.   Palmer, B.J. (1950). *Up from below the bottom*, p. 504.

2.   Ibid, p. 448.

Chapter 11

1.   Palmer, B.J. (1950). *Fight to climb*, pp. 92-3.

2.   Palmer, B.J. (1966). *Our masterpiece.* Davenport, IA: PSC, p. 135.

Chapter 12

1.   Palmer, B.J. (1958). *Palmer's law of life*, p. 33.

Chapter 13

1.   Palmer, B.J. (1958). *Palmer's law of life*, p. 12.

2.   Palmer, B.J. (1955). *Chiropractic philosophy: Science, and art: what it does, how it does it, and why it does it.* Davenport, IA: PSC, p. 56.

Chapter 14

1.   Palmer, B.J. (1949). *The bigness of fellow within*, p. 57.

Chapter 15

1.   Palmer, B.J. (1955). *Chiropractic philosophy*, p. 25.

2.   Palmer, B.J. (1957). *Evolution or revolution*, p. 39.

3.   Palmer, B.J. (1951). *Clinical controlled chiropractic research.* Hammond, Indiana: Conkey Co., p. 209.

3.   Palmer, B.J. (1966). *Our masterpiece*, p. 131.

Chapter 16

1.   Palmer, B.J. (1949). *The bigness of fellow within*, p. 21.

2.   Palmer, B.J. (1950). *Up from below the bottom*, p. 200.

3.   Ibid, p. 842.

Chapter 17

1.   Palmer, B.J. (1957). *Evolution or revolution*, p. 49.

2.   Palmer, B.J. (1958). *Palmer's law of life*, p. 102.

3.   Palmer, B.J. (1957). *Evolution or revolution*, p. 63.

Chapter 18

1. Palmer, D.D. (1910). *The chiropractor's adjuster*. Portland: Portland Printing Company, p. 393.

2. Palmer, B.J. (1966). *The great divide*. Davenport: IA, p. 6.

3. Palmer, B.J. (1961). *The glory of going on*, p. 38.

Chapter 19

1. Palmer, B.J. (1949). *The bigness of fellow within*, p. 125.

2. Palmer, B.J. (1955). *Chiropractic philosophy*, p. 8.

Chapter 20

1. Palmer, B.J. (1961). *The glory of going on*, p. 79.

2. Palmer, B.J. (1950). *Up from below the bottom*, p. 18.

Chapter 21

1. Palmer, B.J. (1949). *The bigness of fellow within*, pp. viii-x.

2. Palmer, B.J. (1966). *Our masterpiece*, pp. 125-126.

Chapter 22

1. Palmer, B.J. (1949). *The bigness of fellow within*, pp. 47-48.

2. Palmer, B.J. (1957). *Evolution or revolution*, p. 93.

3. Ibid, p. 93.

Chapter 23

1. Palmer, B.J. (1950). *Up from below the bottom*, p. 30.

2. Palmer, B.J. (1958). *Palmer's law of life*, p. 15.

3. From a talk delivered at ALL-SCHOOL ASSEMBLY, June 8th, 1960. Palmer, B.J. (1961). *The glory of going on*, p. 81

Epilogue

1. Graves, C. (1974). Human nature prepares for a momentous leap. *The Futurist*, 1974, 72-87.

    Beck, D., Cowan, C. (1996). *Spiral dynamics*. Oxford: Blackwell Publishers.

2. Loevinger, J. (1976). *Ego development*. San Francisco: Jossey-Bass. Cook-Greuter, S. (1999). Postautonomous ego development[Dissertation]. Ann Arbor: UMI.

3. Commons, M., Richards, F, Armon, C. (Eds.) (1984). Beyond formal operations: Late adolescent and adult cognitive development. NY: Praeger.

Aurobindo, S. (2005). *The life divine. Volume 21 & 22; The complete works of Sri Aurobindo*. Pondicherry, India: Sri Aurobindo Ashram Publication Dept.

4.   Fowler, J.W. (1995). *Stages of faith: The psychology of human development and the quest for meaning*. San Francisco: HarperCollins.

5.   Wilber, K. (2000). *Integral psychology*. Boston: Shambhala.

6.   Gebser J. (1949). *The ever present origin*. Athens: Ohio University Press.
Wilber, K. (2003). *Excerpt A*. Kosmos.
Senzon, SA. (2007). *Chiropractic foundations*.

7.   Wilber, K. (1995). *Sex ecology and spirituality*. Boston: Shambhala.

8.   Wilber, K. (2006). *Integral Spirituality*. Boston: Shambhala.
Esbjörn-Hargens, S. (2009). An overview of integral theory. Integral Inst.

9.   Palmer, D.D. (1910). *The chiropractor's adjuster*.
Palmer, B.J. (1949). *The bigness of the fellow within*.

10.   Palmer, D.D. (1910). *The chiropractor's adjuster*. Palmer, B.J. (1958). *Palmer's law of life*. Senzon, S.A. (2007). *Chiropractic foundations*.

11.   Keating, J. (1997). *B.J. of Davenport*. Davenport, Iowa: AHC.
Maynard, J.E. (1982). *Healing hands*. MS: Jonorm Publishers.
Senzon, SA. (2004). *The spiritual writings of B.J. Palmer: The second chiropractor*. Asheville, NC: Self published.

12.   Wardwell, W. (1992). *Chiropractic: Evolution of a new profession*.
Moore, J.S. (1993). *Chiropractic in America: The history of a medical alternative*. Johns Hopkins Univ. Press. Gaucher, L. (1993). *Chiropractic: Early concepts in their historical setting*. Chicago: National College. Peterson, D., Wiese, G. (1995). *Chiropractic: An illustrated history*. St. Louis: Mosby.

13.   Senzon, SA. (2000). An integral approach to unifying the philosophy of chiropractic: B.J. Palmer's model of consciousness. *Journal of Integral Studies*, Issue 2. Senzon, SA. (2001). A History of the *mental impulse*: Theoretical construct or scientific reality. *Chiropractic History*, 21(2), 63-76. Senzon, SA. (2004). *The spiritual writings of B.J. Palmer*. Senzon, SA. (2005). *The secret*

history of chiropractic: D.D. Palmer's spiritual writings. Senzon, SA. (2007). *Chiropractic foundations.*

14. Moore, J.S. (1993). *Chiropractic in America.* Albanese, C. (2007). *A republic of mind and spirit: A cultural history of American metaphysical religion.* New Haven: Yale Univ. Press. Senzon, SA. (2007). *Chiropractic foundations.*

15. Senzon, SA. (2007). *Chiropractic foundations.*

16. Wilber, K. (1998). *The marriage of sense and soul.* Boston: Shambhala. Senzon, SA. (2005). *The secret history of chiropractic.* Senzon, SA. (2007). *Chiropractic foundations.*

17. Pauchant, T. (2005). Integral leadership: a research proposal. *Journal of Organizational Change Management,* 18(3), 211-229.

18. Volckmann, R. (2004). A fresh perspective: Integral leadership: The 100 book project, an excerpt from a conversation with Thierry C. Pauchant. *Integral Leadership Review,* IV(4).

19. Pauchant, T. (2005). Integral Leadership. Volckmann, R. (2004). A fresh perspective.

20. Pauchant, T. (2005). Integral Leadership.

21. Pauchant, T. (2004). Methodology: Requirements and guide to Nvivo. Pauchant, T. (2005). Integral Leadership.

22. Bennis, W.G., Thomas, R.J. (2002), "Crucibles of leadership", *Harvard Business Review,* 80, 39-45.

23. Denzin N. (1994). The art and politics of interpretation, p. 510.

24. Pauchant, T. (2005). Integral Leadership. Wilber, K. (2006). *Integral Spirituality.* Developmental survey instruments are ways that developmental psychologists can measure an individual's development in several lines such as cognitive, values, spirituality, morals, etc.

25. Stein, Z. (2008). Intuitions of altitude: Researching the conditions of the possibility for developmental assessment. *1st Biennial Integral Theory Conference,* Pleasant Hill, CA. August 2008. Pleasant Hill, Ca.

26. Pauchant, T. (2004). The leadographies on integral development.

27.   Lerner, C. (1952). *The Lerner report.* Davenport: Palmer College Archives. Moore, J.S. (1993). *Chiropractic in America.* Gaucher, L. (1993). *Chiropractic: Early concepts.* Peterson, D., Wiese, G. (1995). *Chiropractic: An illustrated history.* Gibbons, R.W. (1987). Assessing the oracle at the Fountainhead: B.J. Palmer and his times, 1902-1961. *Chiropractic History*, 7(1), 8-14. Gibbons, RW. (1994). "With malice aforethought": Revisiting the B.J. Palmer "patricide" controversy. *Chiropractic History*, 14(1), 28-34. Quigley, W. (1989). The last days of B.J. Palmer: Revolutionary confronts reality. *Chiropractic History*, 9(2), 11-19.

28.   Keating, J. (1997). *B.J. of Davenport.*

29.   Palmer, D. (1967). *The Palmers.* Davenport IA: Bawden Brothers. Panza, E. (1982). *The life and times of B.J. Palmer.* Williamsburg VA. Senzon, SA. (2004). *The spiritual writings of B.J. Palmer.* Maynard, J.E. (1982). *Healing hands.* Dye, A. (1939). *The evolution of chiropractic: Its discovery and development.* Philadelphia: A.E. Dye.

30.   Senzon, SA. (2001). A History of the mental impulse. Senzon, SA. (2004). *The spiritual writings of B.J. Palmer.*

31.   Palmer, B.J. (1949). *The bigness of fellow within.* Palmer, B.J. (1950). *Up from below the bottom.* Palmer, B.J. (1950). *Fight to climb.* (1951). *Clinical controlled chiropractic research.* Davenport, IA: PSC. Palmer, B.J. (1951). *Conflicts clarify.* Davenport, IA: PSC. Palmer, B.J. (1951). *History repeats.* Davenport, IA: PSC. Palmer, B.J. (1952). *Answers.* Palmer, B.J. (1953). *Upside down inside out with B.J.* Davenport, IA: PSC. Palmer, B.J. (1955). *Chiropractic philosophy.* Palmer, B.J. (1955). *Fame and fortune.* Davenport, IA: PSC. Palmer, B.J. (1957). *Evolution or revolution.* Palmer, B.J. (1957). *History in the making.* Davenport, IA: Palmer College. Palmer, B.J. (1958). *Palmer's law of life.* Palmer, B.J. (1961). *The glory of going on.* Palmer, B.J. (1966). The *great divide.* Palmer, B.J. (1966). *Our masterpiece.*

32.   Quigley, W. (1989). The last days of B.J. Palmer.

33. Allen, L. (1990). "I owed my life to this strange profession." *Today's Chiropractic*, 19(6). 20. Barge, F. (1990). Did I Know B.J. Palmer? *Today's Chiropractic*, 19(6), 38. Crowder, E. (1990). B.J. the Rainmaker: A Giver, Not a Taker. *Today's Chiropractic*, 19(6), 28. Peet, H. (1990). Our lives entwined with Dr. B.J. Palmer. *Today's Chiropractic*, 19(6), 26. Rutherford. (1990). B.J. - The man I knew. *Today's Chiropractic*, 19(6), 24. Williams, S. (1990). Lyceum: Crossing The River. *Today's Chiropractic*, 19(6), 7.

34. Maynard, J.E. (1990). The passing of a healer. *Today's Chiropractic*, 19 (6).

35. Cook-Greuter, S. (1999). Postautonomous ego development.

36. Cook-Greuter, S. (2004). Personal communication.

37. Wilber, K. (2006). *Integral Spirituality*, p. ix.

38. Wilber, K. (2006). *Integral Spirituality*.

39. Pauchant, T. (2005). Integral Leadership.

40. Wilber, K. (2006). *Integral Spirituality*.

41. Maynard, J.E. (1982). *Healing hands*. Keating, J. (1997). *B.J. of Davenport*. Palmer, B.J. (1949). *The bigness of fellow within*.

42. Wilber, K. (2000). *Integral psychology*.

43. Ibid.

44. Volckmann, R. (2004). A fresh perspective.

45. Bennis, W.G., Thomas, R.J. (2002). "Crucibles of leadership", p. 40.

46. Thomas, R. (2002). The crucible of leadership. *Human Performance Insights*, 1:1-4.

47. Palmer, B.J. (1950). *Fight to climb*.

48. Maynard, J.E. (1982). *Healing hands*.

49. Keating, J. (1997). *B.J. of Davenport*.

50. Lerner, C. (1952). *The Lerner report*, p.52.

51. Lerner, C. (1952). *The Lerner report*.
     Senzon, S.A. (2004). *The spiritual writings of B.J. Palmer*.

52. Palmer, B.J. (1949). *The bigness of fellow within*, p. xix. Palmer, B.J. (1950). *Fight to climb*, p. 65. Palmer, B.J. (1952). *Answers*, p. 79. Palmer, B.J. (1961). *The glory of going on*, p. 56. Palmer, B.J. (1966). Our masterpiece, p. 116.

53.   Thomas, R. (2002). The crucible of leadership.

54.   Lerner, C. (1952). *The Lerner report.*

55.   Senzon, SA. (2004). *The spiritual writings of B.J. Palmer.*

56.   Palmer, B.J. (1966). Our masterpiece, p. 116.

57.   Lerner, C. (1952). *The Lerner report.*

58.   Wilber, K. (2000). *Integral psychology, p. 59.* Wade, J. (1996). *Changes of mind: A holonomic theory of the evolution of consciousness.* Albany, NY: SUNY Press.

60.   Cook-Greuter, S. (1990). Maps for living: Ego-development stages from symbiosis to conscious universal embeddedness.

61.   Peterson, D., Wiese, G. (1995). *Chiropractic: An illustrated history.*

62.   Gibbons, R.W. (1987). Assessing the oracle
Keating, J. (1997). *B.J. of Davenport.*

63.   Gibbons, R.W. (1987). Assessing the oracle.
Keating, J. (1997). *B.J. of Davenport.*

64.   Gibbons, RW. (1994). "With malice aforethought."

65.   Keating, J., Troyanovich, S. (2005). Wisconsin versus chiropractic: the trials at LaCrosse and the birth of a chiropractic champion. *Chiropractic History,* 25(1): 37-45.

66.   Wiese, G. (2003). With head, heart, and hands.

67.   Palmer, B.J. (1952). *Answers.* Gromola, T. (1985). Broadsides & epigrams.

68.   Keating, J. (1997). *B.J. of Davenport.* Bower N., Hynes R. (2004). Going to jail for chiropractic: A career's defining moment. *Chiropractic History,* 24(2), 21-25. Callender, A. (2004). B.J. Palmer, the Universal Chiropractic Association, and Civil Disobedience. *Chiropractic History,* 24(2), 75-80.

69.   Palmer, B.J. (1952). *Answers.* pp. 308, 312.

70.   Linhart, G. (1988). Selling the "Big Idea": B.J. Palmer ushers in the golden age, 1906-1920. *Chiropractic History,* 8(2), 25-30.
Keating, J. (1997). *B.J. of Davenport.*

71.   Quigley, W. (1989). The last days of B.J. Palmer, p. 11.

72.   Thomas, R. (2002). The crucible of leadership.

73.   Quigley, W. (1989). The last days of B.J. Palmer.
      Keating, J. (1997). *B.J. of Davenport.*

74.   Mork, E. (1990). Learning from Dr. B.J. Palmer. *Today's Chiropractic*, 19 (6).

75.   Thomas, R. (2002). The crucible of leadership. Palmer, B.J. (1926). *'Round the world with B.J. Palmer.* Davenport, IA: PSC. Palmer, B.J. (1953). *Upside down inside out with B.J.* Davenport, IA: PSC.

77.   Palmer, B.J. (1951). *Clinical controlled chiropractic research.* Davenport: PSC.

78.   Gaucher, L. (1993). *Chiropractic: Early concepts.* Senzon, SA. (2005). *The secret history of chiropractic.* Senzon, SA. (2007). *Chiropractic foundations.* Callender, AK. (2007). The mechanistic/vitalistic dualism of chiropractic and general systems theory: Daniel D. Palmer and Ludwig von Bertalanffy. *Journal of Chiropractic Humanities*, 14(1), 1-21.

79.   Palmer, B.J. (1950). *Up from below the bottom.*

80.   Commons, M., et al. (1984). (eds.) *Beyond formal operations.*

81.   Cook-Greuter, S. (1999). Postautonomous ego development. Cook-Greuter, S. (2004). Making the case for a developmental perspective. *Industrial and Commercial Training*, 36(7), 275-281. Ingersoll, E., Cook-Greuter, S. (2007). The self-system in integral counseling. *Counseling and Values*, 51(3), 193-208.

82.   Cook-Greuter, S. (1999). Postautonomous ego development.

83.   Beck, D., Cowan, C. (1996). *Spiral dynamics.*

84.   Dye, A. (1939). *The evolution of chiropractic*, p. 293.

85.   Palmer, B.J. (1936). (1936). The *known man or an explanation of the "phenomenon of life".* Davenport, IA: PSC. Palmer, B.J. (1951). *Clinical controlled chiropractic research.* Senzon, S.A. (2001). A History of the mental impulse. Senzon, S.A. (2008). Chiropractic and energy medicine: A shared history. *Journal of Chiropractic Humanities*: 15, 27-54.

86.   Palmer, B.J. (1949). *The bigness of fellow within*, p. 32.

87.   Wilber, K. (2006). *Integral Spirituality.*
      Senzon, SA. (2007). *Chiropractic foundations.*

88.   Palmer, B.J. (1953). *Upside down inside out.*
      Palmer, B.J. (1966). *Our masterpiece.*

89.   Palmer, B.J. (1949). *The bigness of fellow within.*

90.   Quigley, W. (1989). The last days of B.J. Palmer.

91.   Commons, M., et al. (1984). (eds.) *Beyond formal operations.*

92.   Aurobindo, S. (2005). *The life divine.*

93.   Cook-Greuter, S. (1999). Postautonomous ego development.

94.   Cook-Greuter, S. (2004). Making the case for a developmental perspective.

95.   Palmer, B.J. (1953). *Upside down inside out.*

96.   Cook-Greuter, S. (2004). Making the case for a developmental perspective.

97.   Fowler, J.W. (1995). *Stages of faith.*

98.   Fowler, J.W. (1995). *Stages of faith*, pp. 199-201.

99.   Palmer, B.J. (1949). *The bigness of fellow within.* Palmer, B.J. (1955). *Chiropractic philosophy.* Palmer, B.J. (1966). *Our masterpiece.*

100.   Wade, J. (1996). *Changes of mind*, p.163.

101.   Pauchant, T. (2005). Integral Leadership.

102.   Palmer, B.J. (1958). *Palmer's law of life.*
        Maynard, J.E. (1982). *Healing hands.*

103.   Aurobindo, S. (2005). *The life divine.*

104.   Palmer, B.J. (1955). *Chiropractic philosophy*, p. 116.

105.   Maynard, J.E. (1982). *Healing hands.*

106.   Luckey, W. (1961). Dr. B.J. Palmer dies at age 79; called Developer of chiropractic. *Digest of Chiropractic Economics*, 3(6), 23,31.
        Bach, M. (1968). *The chiropractic story.* Los Angeles: DeVorss.

107.   Pauchant, T. (2005). Integral leadership.

108.   Bach, M. (1968). *The chiropractic story*, pp.159-161.

109.   Ibid, p. 161.

110.   Wilber, K. (2006). *Integral Spirituality.*

111.   Palmer, B.J. (1955). *Chiropractic philosophy*, p. 48.

112.   Palmer, B.J. (1961). *The glory of going on*, p. 261.

113.   Luckey, W. (1961). Dr. B.J. Palmer dies at age 79.

114.   Maynard, J.E. (1982). *Healing hands*, p.191.

Appendix A

1. Allen, L. (1990). "I owed my life to this strange profession."

2. Barge, F. (1990). Did I Know B.J. Palmer?

3. Crowder, E. (1990). B.J. the Rainmaker: A Giver, Not a Taker.

4. Peet, H. (1990). Our lives entwined with Dr. B.J. Palmer.

5. Rutherford. (1990). B.J. - The man I knew.

6. Williams, S. (1990). Lyceum: Crossing The River.

Appendix B

1. Cook-Greuter, S. (2004). Personal Communication.

Bibliography

Albanese, C. (2007). *A republic of mind and spirit: A cultural history of American metaphysical religion.* New Haven: Yale University Press.

Allen, L. (1990). "I owed my life to this strange profession." *Today's Chiropractic*, 19(6), 20.

Aurobindo, S. (2005). *The life divine. Volume 21 & 22; The complete works of Sri Aurobindo.* Pondicherry, India: Sri Aurobindo Ashram Publication Department.

Bach, M. (1968). *The chiropractic story.* Los Angeles: DeVorss.

Barge, F. (1990). Did I Know B.J. Palmer? *Today's Chiropractic*, 19(6), 38.

Beck, D., Cowan, C. (1996). *Spiral dynamics: Mastering values, leadership, and change.* Oxford: Blackwell Publishers.

Bennis, W.G., Thomas, R.J. (2002), "Crucibles of leadership", *Harvard Business Review*, 80, 39-45.

Bower N., Hynes R. (2004). Going to jail for chiropractic: A career's defining moment. *Chiropractic History*, 24(2), 21-25.

Brown, B. (2007). Blazing the trail from infancy to enlightenment; parts 1-3. Boulder: Integral Institute.

Callender, A. (2004). B.J. Palmer, the Universal Chiropractic Association, and Civil Disobedience. *Chiropractic History*, 24(2), 75-80.

Callender, AK. (2007). The mechanistic/vitalistic dualism of chiropractic and general systems theory: Daniel D. Palmer and Ludwig von Bertalanffy. *Journal of Chiropractic Humanities*, 14(1), 1-21.

Cook-Greuter, S. (1990). Maps for living: Ego-development stages from symbiosis to conscious universal embeddedness. In Commons, M., Armon, C. Kohlberg, L., Richards, F., Grotzner, T., Sinnott, J.

(Eds.). *Adult development; volume 2: Models and Methods in the study of adolescent and adult thought*. New York: Praeger.

Cook-Greuter, S. (2004b). Personal communication.

Commons, M., Richards, F, Armon, C. (Eds.) (1984). *Beyond formal operations: Late adolescent and adult cognitive development*. New York: Praeger.

Crowder, E. (1990). B.J. the Rainmaker: A Giver, Not a Taker. *Today's Chiropractic*, 19(6), 28.

Denzin N. (1994). The art and politics of interpretation. In: Denzin, N, Lincoln Y. (eds). (1994). *Handbook of qualitative research*. Thousand Oaks: Sage Publications.

Dye, A. (1939). *The evolution of chiropractic: Its discovery and development*. Philadelphia: A.E. Dye.

Esbjörn-Hargens S. (2009). An overview of integral theory: An all inclusive framework for the 21st century [resource paper no. 1]. Integral Institute 2009;1–24. Accessed April 8, 2009: www.integrallife.com

Fowler, J.W. (1995). *Stages of faith: The psychology of human development and the quest for meaning*. San Francisco: HarperCollins.

Gaucher, P.L. (1993). *Chiropractic: Early concepts in their historical setting*. Chicago: National College of Chiropractic.

Gebser, J. (1949). *The ever present origin*. Athens: Ohio University Press.

Gelardi, T. (1999). *Inspirations*. Spartanburg, SC: Sherman College.

Gibbons, R.W. (1987). Assessing the oracle at the Fountainhead: B.J. Palmer and his times, 1902-1961. *Chiropractic History*, 7(1), 8-14.

Gibbons, RW. (1994). "With malice aforethought": Revisiting the B.J. Palmer "patricide" controversy. *Chiropractic History*, 14(1), 28-34.

Graves, C. Human nature prepares for a momentous leap. *The Futurist*, 1974, 72-87.

Gromola, T. (1985). Broadsides, Epigrams, and Testimonials: The Evolution of Chiropractic Advertising. *Chiropractic History*, 4(1), 41-45.

Hubbard, E. (1911). *A thousand & one epigrams: Selected from the writings of Elbert Hubbard*. East Aurora: Roycrofters.

Ingersoll, E., Cook-Greuter, S. (2007). The self-system in integral counseling. *Counseling and Values*, 51(3), 193-208.

Keating, J. (1997). *B.J. of Davenport: The early years of chiropractic*. Davenport, Iowa: Association for the History of Chiropractic.

Keating, J, Troyanovich, S. (2005). Wisconsin versus chiropractic: the trials at LaCrosse and the birth of a chiropractic champion. *Chiropractic History*, 25(1), 37-45.

Kegan, R., Noam, G., & Rogers L. (1982). The psychologic of emotion: A Neo-Piagetian view. In Cicchetti, D., Hess, P. (Eds.) *New directions for child development: Emotional development*. San Francisco: Jossey-Bass.

Kohlberg, L. (1981). *The philosophy of moral development*, pp. 409-412. Quoted in Brown, B. (2007). Blazing the trail from infancy to enlightenment. Unpublished manuscript.

Lerner, C. (1952). *The Lerner report*. Palmer College Archives: Davenport, IA.

Linhart, G. (1988). Selling the "Big Idea": B.J. Palmer ushers in the golden age, 1906-1920. *Chiropractic History*, 8(2), 25-30.

Luckey, W. (1961). Dr. B.J. Palmer dies at age 79; called Developer of chiropractic. *Digest of Chiropractic Economics*, 3(6), 23; 31.

Loevinger, J. (1976). *Ego development*. San Francisco: Jossey-Bass.

Martin, S. 1993. Chiropractic and the social context of medical technology, 1895-1925 *Technology and Culture*, 34(4), 808-834.

Maynard, J.E. (1982). *Healing hands: The story of the Palmer family discoverers and developers of chiropractic. Revised edition.* MS: Jonorm Publishers.

Maynard, J.E. (1990). The passing of a healer. *Today's Chiropractic,* 19 (6).

Moore, J.S. (1993). *Chiropractic in America: The history of a medical alternative.* Johns Hopkins University Press.

Mork, E. (1990). Learning from Dr. B.J. Palmer. *Today's Chiropractic,* 19(6), 46.

Nixon, P. 1927. *Martial and the modern epigram.* New York: Longmans, Green and Co.

Palmer, B.J. (1911). *The philosophy and principles of chiropractic adjustments: A series of thirty eight lectures.* Davenport, IA: Palmer College.

Palmer, B.J. (1920). *A textbook on the Palmer technique of chiropractic.* Davenport, IA: Palmer College.

Palmer, B.J. (1926). *'Round the world with B.J. Palmer.* Davenport, IA: Palmer College.

Palmer, B.J. (1934). *The Subluxation specific the adjustment specific.* Davenport. IA: Palmer College.

Palmer, B.J. (1936). The *known man or an explanation of the "phenomenon of life".* Davenport, IA: Palmer College.

Palmer, B.J. (1947). 6th ed. *Radio salesmanship.* Davenport, IA:PSC Press.

Palmer, B.J. (1949). *The Bigness of the fellow within.* Davenport, IA: Palmer College.

Palmer, B.J. (1950). *Up from below the bottom.* Palmer College, Davenport, IA.

Palmer, B.J. (1950). *Fight to climb.* Davenport, IA: Palmer College.

Palmer, B.J. (1951). *Clinical controlled chiropractic research.* Davenport, IA: Palmer College.

Palmer, B.J. (1951). *Conflicts clarify.* Davenport, IA: Palmer College.

Palmer, B.J. (1951). *History repeats*. Davenport, IA: Palmer College

Palmer, B.J. (1952). *Answers*. Davenport, IA: Palmer College.

Palmer, B.J. (1953). *Upside down inside out with B.J.* Davenport, IA: Palmer College.

Palmer, B.J. (1955b). *Chiropractic philosophy. science, and art: what it does, how it does it, and why it does it*. vol. 32. Davenport, IA: Palmer College.

Palmer, B.J. (1955). *Fame and fortune*. Davenport, IA: Palmer College.

Palmer, B.J. (1957). *Evolution or revolution*. Davenport, IA: Palmer College.

Palmer, B.J. (1957). *History in the making*. Davenport, IA: Palmer College.

Palmer, B.J. (1958). *Palmer's law of life*. Davenport, IA: Palmer College.

Palmer, B.J. (1961). *The glory of going on*. Davenport, IA: Palmer College.

Palmer, B.J. (1966). The *great divide*. Davenport, IA: Palmer College.

Palmer, B.J. (1966). *Our masterpiece*. Davenport, IA: Palmer College.

Palmer, B.J. (1988). *As a man thinketh*. Davenport, Iowa: Delta Sigma Chi.

Palmer College website: B.J. Palmer's epigrams. Retrieved Nov 22, 2009 from: http://www.palmer.edu/history2.aspx?id=1142

Palmer, D.D. (1910). *The chiropractor's adjuster*. Portland: Portland Printing Company.

Pauchant, T. (2005). Integral leadership: a research proposal. *Journal of Organizational Change Management*, 18(3), 211-229.

Pauchant, T. (2004a). Methodology: Requirements and guide to Nvivo. Retrieved March 2, 2010, from: http://web.hec.ca/leadergraphies/dropdown/intro.htm#

Pauchant, T. (2004b). The leadographies on integral development: Commented outline. Retrieved March 2, 2010, from http://web.hec.ca/leadergraphies/dropdown/leadergraphies_series.ht m

Palmer, D. (1967). *The Palmers*. Davenport IA: Bawden Brothers.

Panza, E. (1982). *The life and times of B.J. Palmer.* Williamsburg VA: E. Panza.

Peet, H. (1990). Our lives entwined with Dr. B.J. Palmer. *Today's Chiropractic,* 19(6), 26.

Peterson, D., Wiese, G. (1995). Chiropractic; An illustrated history. St. Louis: Mosby.

Quigley, W. (1989). The last days of B.J. Palmer: Revolutionary confronts reality. *Chiropractic History,* 9(2), 11-19.

Rehm, W.S., (1986). Legally defensible: Chiropractic in the courtroom and after, 1907.*Chiropractic History,* 6, 51.

Rutherford. (1990). B.J. - The man I knew. *Today's Chiropractic,* 19(6), 24.

Senzon, SA. (2000). An integral approach to unifying the philosophy of chiropractic: B.J. Palmer's model of consciousness. *Journal of Integral Studies.* Issue 2.

Senzon, SA. (2001). A History of the *mental impulse*; Theoretical construct or scientific reality. *Chiropractic History,* 21(2), 63-76.

Senzon, SA. (2004). *The spiritual writings of B.J. Palmer: The second chiropractor.* Asheville, NC: Self published.

Senzon, SA. (2005). *The secret history of chiropractic: D.D. Palmer's spiritual writings.* Asheville, NC: Self published.

Senzon, SA. (2007). *Chiropractic foundations: D.D. Palmer's traveling library.* Asheville, NC: Self published.

Senzon, SA. (2008). Chiropractic and energy medicine: A shared history. *Journal of Chiropractic Humanities*: 15, 27-54.

Stechschulte, P. (2008). The writing on the wall new epigrams for Life University. *Today's Chiropractic Lifestyle,* Feb/Mar, 62-64.